What Do You Say to a ... Naked Icebox?

A Cookbook for College Students and Other Kitchen Virgins

by

Pamela Smith Connolly

DORRANCE PUBLISHING CO., INC.
PITTSBURGH, PENNSYLVANIA 15222

All Rights Reserved
Copyright © 1997 by Pamela Smith Connolly
No part of this book may be reproduced or transmitted
in any form or by any means, electronic or mechanical,
including photocopying, recording, or by any information
storage and retrieval system without permission in
writing from the publisher.

ISBN # 0-8059-4178-9
Printed in the United States of America

First Printing

For information or to order additional books, please write:
Dorrance Publishing Co., Inc.
643 Smithfield Street
Pittsburgh, PA 15222
U.S.A.

*Dedicated, with love, to my son Michael,
my daughter Elizabeth and all of the others
who have grown up as "kitchen virgins" believing
that cooking involves some arcane magic
known only to middle aged mothers.*

*And, of course, to Mike,
my best friend in Claremont.*

A Mother's Philosophy of Eating

*"To everything there is a season and a time
for every purpose under heaven."*
—Eccles. 3:1.

Your purpose, which you have accepted by buying this book for your kitchen library, is to occasionally COOK!

Try it. You may like it and even find it a creative way to keep body and soul together!

This Mother's Food Philosophy:

I don't believe in starving students, starving artists, or starving anyones! I also don't believe in chicken soup, so you won't find a recipe for it in this book. I do believe we all think better when we have good food and a good night's sleep. So why not cook what you like yourself? Ask your own mother for some of your favorite recipes and write them in the "Family Album" pages at the end of this book. Then anywhere you find yourself will be "home" when you are in the kitchen.

Food is love, so love yourself and
HAVE FUN!!

*Love,
Mom*

The Semester Plan

FALL
: Keep it simple! Warm weather...BBQ, Salads, and nuked food.

BEFORE MID-TERMS
: Write your mother and/or father. Get them on your side before grades come out. (This is also a good time to ask for a little extra money if you need it.)

THANKSGIVING VACATION
: Pack up and GO! The icebox will miss you but not become hostile because of rejection.

FINALS
: Soups, stews, chili, store-bought lasagna, and your own freezer meals. Start cleaning out the fridge!

CHRISTMAS VACATION
: Really clean out the icebox, or when you get back it will have turned ugly on you. Yes, penicillin was discovered on moldy lemons, but the slime that will await you from those six leaves of lettuce you left in the crisper drawer can be worse than any sci-fi horror film Hollywood has ever created, especially because YOU have to deal with them.

WINTER
: Numero uno restock the icebox and the shelves with the essentials! Think good hearty foods for cold weather: spaghetti, meat loaf, casseroles, chili, and hot sandwiches. STUDY! Party! WORK! Party! STUDY!

MID-TERMS
: See FALL....

FINALS
: Keep it simple and easy on the clean up. It's a real temptation to just dump things in the sink to harden beyond redemption while you virtuously scurry back to your books and papers.

DO NOT DO THIS!

Contents

Basic Definitions vii
Recipe Key viii
Notes On "Sharing" an Icebox ix
Shelf-Stocking 101 x
The Cold vs. the Hard Facts Of Life 2
Tools Of the Trade 5
Hamburger Doesn't Need Help! 12
Foolproof Fowl 21
The Anatomy Of the Rib 29
Pig In 34
Ichthyology 41
Primary Pasta 47
Independent Studies In Starches 52
Impress the Guests with a Dead Hot Dog and Other Lovable Leftovers 60
Your Future In Menu Management 75
Your Own Favorite Menus 77
Index 78
Family Album (Your Own Recipes) 81

Basic Definitions

Icebox: *a.k.a. Refrigerator, reefer, fridge (idaire-ask your grandparents.)* **1.** An electrical kitchen unit that keeps your food cold or frozen in separate compartments and thus keeps it from spoiling and killing you, your roommates, or guests. **2.** An archaic piece of kitchen furniture that your forefathers and mothers used to fill with blocks of old lake ice....it now holds a lamp, a potted plant, and a tasteful ashtray in your Aunt Emmadine's front hall. **3.** Your life line between institutional food, plastic food, and total indebtedness to fast food at outrageous costs to both your health and your pocketbook and real food. **4.** An excellent source of samples for interesting biology projects.

Freezer: The smaller part of the icebox that keeps ice cubes and ice cream in a solid state. When only one or two are normally gathered together to create food, a place of short-term investment, with diminishing interest over the long haul.

Kitchen Virgins: **1.** Future chefs who have not yet begun to cook. **2.** Those people who have not yet looked beyond an article of food as a momentary urge—the peanut butter, ice cream or potato chip cravings—and have limited their "cooking" to zapping microwave popcorn or mini-pizza.

Recipe: **1.** A time-honored formula for putting various foods together to form a reasonably edible whole. **2.** One person's palate-pleasing delicacy so honored as to appear at every potluck until everyone this person knows vows not to attend another potluck until after the funeral. **3.** The contents of this book. Trust a mother—all of these "formulas" are easier to understand and more palatable than $E=MC^2$

Cooking: Preparing food for eating.

Recipe Key

M	Microwavable. Foods that are suitable for cooking, or reheating, in a very short time by molecular disturbance.
F & E	Fast & Easy. Perfect for a snack or a meal during times of stress, like final exams or the take-home project that could make or break your raise/promotion. Also good when your significant other's mother calls from the airport to let you know she is just waiting for the rental car and will be at your place for dinner. These can be made from the basic cupboard and icebox essentials that you "always" have on hand.
E:	Easy. Takes a little preparation and cooking time. May need some prior shopping for a few of the ingredients.
MC:	Moderately Challenging. These recipes may require some thought, shopping, and timing. Good for a dinner or weekend when you feel like creative procrastination for a worthy cause—your mental health—or when you realize that your taste buds have actually come to accept cafeteria food as real food.
TLC:	Time, Love, and Care. For those rare times when you really have time or are simply bored out of your skull. Not necessarily complicated recipes but those that need to be watched over or involve several timed steps to prepare.
FFC:	Fit For Company. May be F & E, E, MC, or TLC but can be dressed up and presented like you've spent hours in the kitchen. (Note: Don't try to fool your mother with these. **We know.**) See Impress the Guest.
F-F:	Freezer-Friendly. Some foods can be frozen then thawed and reheated without loss of quality.

Notes on "Sharing" an Icebox

When you are not married, or very closely involved with another person, and are using the same icebox, it can become a hassle. Even old married couples have been known to squabble over whose leftovers are whose! Save yourself the grief by using one, or more, of the following ideas:

Divide the icebox into territorial areas—left and right sides works better than top and bottom because of the drawers.

Color-code containers—yellow is mine, and blue is yours!

Peel-off colored dots—large!

Post 'em notes—but beware, these may need to be taped to stick.

Shelf Stocking 101

Using available shelf and drawer space in a small kitchen could test A.G. Bell's stock of creative inventiveness, but you can organize anything with a little help. One of the world's best inventions are those little plastic turntables available in the cookware section of most big chain markets. Axiom: the bigger the market, the better the selection. But what goes on these little wonders?

MUST-HAVES:

#1

Salt	Pepper	Tabasco Sauce
Parsley Flakes	Chives	Garlic Salt
Chili Powder	Taco Sauce	Liquid Smoke
Ground Cinnamon	Heinz 57 Sauce	

#2

Red Wine Vinegar	Olive Oil	Soy Sauce
Sweet Chili Sauce	Yellow Mustard	Baking Soda
Baking Powder	Maple Syrup	Worcestershire Sauce

Ketchup: You'll probably need a "keg" of this, and it probably won't fit on the little turntable.

Store things near where you'll use them. Try keeping the cutting board near the disposal side of the sink and the sharp knives. A little thinking ahead can save you lots of time when it counts.

Things That Lurk Under The Sink: The best spot for storing dishwashing liquid, paper towels, scouring pads, dishwasher liquid or powder, the dish drainer and rubber mat (Assuming you have limited counter space that you're going to want to use for better things than a collection of drying dishes, pots, and pans.)

Cans that look okay and are acceptable for counter "functional decoration" are called canisters. If you have the available counter space, they can live there or you can put them on a convenient shelf in the cupboard. Use these for storing flour or sugar. If you have to store sugar or flour bags in the shelves, do yourself a big favor and seal them inside ½-gallon or 1-gallon Ziplock bags. They have yet to invent a sack that doesn't leave a fine dusting of flour or sugar on the shelf, and this equals bugs, especially cockroaches and ants. (The only thing known to have a longer life than the cockroach is pasta, which has a longer shelf life than plutonium.)

Stock Those Shelves!

Pam Cooking Spray!

Spaghettini	Cocoa	Noodles Romanoff
Minute Rice	Coffee	Macaroni & Cheese (Box)
Popcorn	Tea	Crackers
Cider Mix	Soups	Instant Mashed Potatoes
Cooking Oils	Sugar	Medium Egg Noodles
Brown Sugar	Flour	Cereals
Pop Tarts		

Canned Goods: Tuna Fish, Sardines, etc.

Anything that doesn't need refrigeration until after it's opened:

Jams	Jellies	Salad Dressings
Salsa	Bean Dip	Chocolate Sauce
Pickles	Chili	Spaghetti Sauce

Hang 'Em High: Some fruits and vegetables stay fresher when air can circulate around them. Try hanging them in a hemp bag for a decorative and practical storage space.

Ideal items are onions, potatoes, avocados, citrus fruits, apples, bananas. Or store them in the colander you use to drain pasta and let it do double duty. (Only store whole fresh fruits and vegetables. Once they have been peeled or cut, they need to be wrapped and put in the icebox.)

Drawers: May be used to store aluminum foil, plastic wrap, and Ziplock bags.

The Cold vs. the Hard Facts of Life

What Do You Say to A Naked Icebox?

"I promise to keep you clean, dust your motor air intake filter, and keep you supplied with a freshly opened box of baking soda every six months if you will promise to keep your cool and not defrost on me without prior notice. And thereto I give you my food."

If you have inherited an abused icebox, clean it with Windex, deodorize and sanitize it with Lysol spray (regular scent...potpourri-scented lettuce is gross), open a box of baking soda and stick it back in a corner, and line the crisper drawers with a double layer of paper toweling. You are now ready to fill your icebox.

Eggs: Usually bought one dozen (twelve) at a time. If you buy these fresh from a reputable source, they don't need refrigeration for five or six days, but since you will probably get these at the market, they'll need to be refrigerated for up to three weeks. **Do not** eat "over the hill" eggs. You will know a bad egg as soon as you crack it by the smell!

Eggs like these are beyond over the hill!

*However, if you are taking psychology or sociology this semester, they are perfect for the maternal bonding project...Congratulations, Mom!

Egg Facts: Fresh eggs will sink in a pan or a bowl of water while eggs laid more than four days previously will float. Eggs can be balanced on end on a flat surface during the equinoxes.

Other Cold Essentials:

Milk	Juice/Punch	Margarine
Bacon	Head Lettuce	Lemon Juice
Mayonnaise	Luncheon Meats	Dressings
American Cheese	Parmesan Cheese	

Optionals: Butter, pickles, horseradish, BBQ sauce, fresh pastas and sauces, and of course LEFTOVERS. Butter is nice to flavor some dishes and for cooking, in combination with margarine or oil, but it is high in cholesterol and expensive, so you'll probably only want to buy half a pound at a time to be used within a month. (Storage hints: small margarine tubs make great leftover keepers and cost nothing compared to buying special storage containers.)

Frozen Solid: Unless you have the national passion for ice cream, the only thing that is absolutely essential in the freezer compartment is ice. It belongs there not only to keep drinks cold but as a first aid necessity! (Ice for a sprain or a nosebleed or a bad bruise; heat for a strain. Ask the PE trainer of an RN to explain the difference, and then join the rest of the world in trying to remember the difference when you need to!)

Optional: Frozen dinners, commercial or homemade (Hint: save the trays from those you may buy to create your own from leftovers and use the microwave to zap them when you need them.) Frozen vegetables, the individual serving boxes equal minimal leftovers and frozen vegetables usually taste better than canned; Frozen Fruits; Fruit Juices; Leftovers; Film, so that it will last beyond the date, but remember to thaw it before you use it; Flashlight Batteries.

Tools of the Trade

Tools

The things with which we cook, ranging from the basic—spoon, bowl, skillet—to the bizarre—cherry pitter, miniature steak timer, cannelloni stuffer, etc. If you are very nice to her, your mother may have a few extra items she's willing to give you for your kitchen. If you have been better than perfect all of your life, she may even take you shopping for what you need, but let's assume you have to start from scratch....

Aluminum Pans: Another great helper of the twentieth century. If you burn food in these, you can recycle them without guilt and at minimal cost. These are especially good for the infrequently used specialty items—muffins and cupcakes, pies, lasagna, a whole chicken, roast, or turkey. They're also great for parties; for example, you can use a big roaster to make a giant green salad for twenty-thirty people. These are available at virtually any market.

Apron: Considered by some to be a sexist item of kitchen apparel worn by women to protect their clothes while cooking but also worn by clever men, especially while barbecuing, covered with cute sayings. Do not ever let a U.S. Navy mess chief think you find him cute or feminine because he wears an apron. Actually, it is a very practical thing for anyone to wear when cooking. Even the world's greatest chefs occasionally get a little messy in the heat of creativity.

Apple Corer: Don't bother buying one of these unless you cannot live without baked apples or plan to go into the apple pie business. They will try to tell you this is also a good peeler but, since that is its secondary function, buy a good peeler instead.

Baster: This can be a brush or a giant eye dropper device that you use to keep meats moist as they cook. The brush or a good-sized spoon are really all you'll need.

Colander: See Strainers.

Bowls: Round ceramic, glass, metal, or wood hollow hemispheres used for everything from holding soup and cereal to mixing, beating, or otherwise combining ingredients efficiently. (If you use a square container, things get caught in the corners, unless you are very careful...)

Mixing Bowls: Can usually be bought in sets of three graduated sizes. Glass

(Pyrex) and metal are the most practical. The former can go in the microwave, and the latter won't break. You might want to get two or three extra small bowls for little jobs and a set of Pyrex custard cups for small melting jobs.

Cookie Sheets: Rimless pieces of metal designed to bake items that are fairly dry or don't become really runny when heated—good for cookies and biscuits but not for scrambled eggs and cake batter. Buy at least two of these (or you can use aluminum).

Fork: An object with two to four prongs called tines, used to stab things and pick them up to transfer them from one area to another; i.e. from the plate to the mouth. Long-handled forks are good for safe cooking over high heat like the BBQ.

Garlic Press: A neat little gismo that has two parts hinged together. The top half has a flat plate, and the bottom half has a small well with holes in it to squish the garlic through. One or two sections (cloves) of peeled garlic should fit into the well. If you really love garlic and find you're using a lot in your cooking, you might want to spend a little extra money and buy a jar of minced or pressed garlic in the produce (vegetable) section of the market and keep it in the icebox, ready to spoon out what you need.

Graters: Tools of varying shapes and sizes designed to turn a solid something—a potato or a block of cheese—into shredded strips of varying lengths and widths.

Griddle: Flat, stovetop cooking surface—sometimes a built-in section of the stove used for grilling and frying basically flat food: bacon, grilled sandwiches, hamburgers, and pancakes. (You can also use a skillet.)

Hot Pads: Your digital saving grace.

Juicers: A. Hand held, B. Counter top model with juice bowl, C. Electrical, D. Industrial. A and B are all you will need unless you decide to compete with Orange Julius. All of these are relatively efficient at extracting juices from citrus fruits.

Knives: Dull for spreading, sharp for cutting, and serrated for sawing through (slicing) bread. (Superstition: if someone gives you a knife, you must "buy" it for a penny or your friendship will be "cut apart.")

Measuring Cups: Cups in 1 cup and 2 cup sizes are really required. Although they are available in plastic and Pyrex, buy the Pyrex so you can microzap in them if you want to. Pitcher: usually plastic with as many gradations as possible. An excellent icebox container for storing juices, iced tea, or other beverages in quantity. Spoons: Absolutely vital! 1T., ½T., 1t.,½t., ¼ t. (⅛t. is a joke! Use the old "pinch" method.) T. = Tablespoon t. = Teaspoon.

Pans: Frying, You'll want a small, a medium, and a large one with a cover, preferably with a non-stick surface.

Sauce, again these are needed in three sizes to accommodate everything from one boiled egg to cooking pasta.

Kettle, *optional*: Although most "Cookbooks" say you need gallons of water for pasta, only the big noodles, like lasagna, really need a kettle.

Specialty, such as omelet, crêpe, and egg poacher. If you like poached eggs you can buy a little one-egg poacher.

Plates: Usually not considered a cooking tool, but in this day of the microwave you can cook whole meals on plates. Paper is cheap and good for nuking bacon and almost any plastic, Pyrex, or white ceramic plate will work. Do not use metal or any plate that has metal trim or a metal-based glaze design unless you hate your microwave.

Roaster: Big, bulky, and hard to store, so if you decide to try roasting a whole turkey, invest in a disposable aluminum pan at the store and recycle it!

Spatulas: Come in three types and you'll want to have at least one of each. A. The soft rubber type on a plastic or wooden handle is for scraping liquids and batters out of bowls and cups or for "folding," gently combining ingredients. B. The flipper type also known as a pancake turner. Metal and heavy plastic are the best. Plastic won't scratch non-stick pans. These also come in wooden shapes which look nice and eco-artsy, but don't work worth a darn. C. The spreader for butter, mayonnaise, and salads.

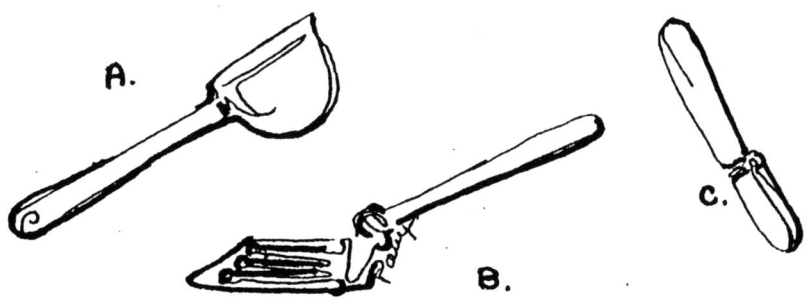

Spoons: Here wood is the best. Slotted spoons are also handy for scooping things, like eggs, out of boiling water or broth.

Strainers: Come in several sizes and shapes for different jobs. Big metal or plastic bowls (colanders) are good for draining pasta or rinsing fruits. Wire baskets are used for submerging foods into frying oil and lifting them out for draining. (Foods cooked this way, such as in fast food shops, are high in saturated fats and usually not economical for home-cooked small batches because they use large amounts of oil.) Bowl-shaped wire mesh baskets on plastic or wooden handles are ideal for draining canned foods and small servings of pasta. These can also be used to "strain" soft, cooked foods, such as an egg yolk or potatoes, and to make baby food by pushing the food through the mesh with the back of a spoon.

Thermometers: Devices for measuring temperature. In cooking these are usually used to check the internal temperature of a large piece of meat (roast beef or a leg of lamb) or a liquid (such as candy, which has to reach a specific temperature to form up when it cools). Various thermometers are designed for specific jobs so don't try to use one for everything.

Tongs: Metal pinchers to pick up hot food—Short-handled for kitchen cooking and long-handled for the BBQ. Also very handy for short people who can't reach boxes and other non-breakables on high shelves.

Vegetable Peeler: Go ahead and buy the cheap metal kind with the handle you can find in any store. When it finally gets dull, as they all do, you won't feel guilty about throwing it away and getting another one.

Whisk: A metal wire "balloon" used to beat foods, like eggs and cream, or to combine ingredients.

You can also buy lots of electrical tools and gadgetry from juicers to mixers, and from graters to waffle irons, but they are all generally more expensive, require careful cleaning, and are usually bulkier, hence harder to store.

Verbal Tools
How to Read and Talk Cooking

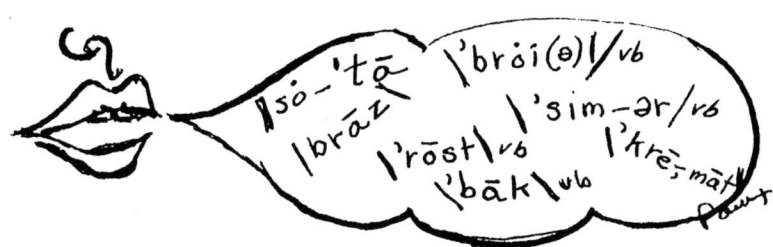

BOILING: To cook in hot water or broth. It seems easy enough, but there are three levels: Simmer, the liquid has little bubbles on the bottom of the pan; Medium boil, when the bubbles keep trying to break the surface, but stirring the liquid with a spoon will stop them for a few moments; Rolling boil, big bubbles constantly breaking the surface that can't be "stirred down."

BRAISE: To cook in liquid at a simmer with the lid on for a long period of time. This long, slow cooking is especially good for tough or stringy cuts of meat. Some recipes will call for doing this on the stove top while others will suggest you use the oven. (a.k.a. stewing)

DICE: Cut into cubes—small, medium, or large.

FRYING: To cook in hot oil or oils. Any oil will burn and eventually catch fire if it gets too hot. Margarine and butter will turn fragrant (light brown), then brown, and then blacken. If you add an equal part of oil to either of these it will take a higher temperature to brown them. As with boiling, frying has three steps: Sauté, to cook gently, usually in butter or margarine at a low to medium heat; Fry, to cook at a medium to high heat to brown or sear the food; and Deep Fry, to totally immerse the food, usually coated in a batter, in hot oil, for a crisp outside and tender inside.

BAKE: To cook in the oven at a moderate temperature, about 350°, with even heat that comes form the heat source at the bottom of the oven. Usually refers to food held in a container like bread or a casserole but it can also mean non-melting foods, like cookies.

BROIL: To cook foods, usually meats, close to the heat source at the top of the oven at a medium-high to high heat. Gas ovens have a separate broiling tray underneath the oven. Because of the high heat, most oven thermostats will shut the heat off unless you crack open the oven door. The food is usually placed on a rack over another pan so that fats and cooking juices don't boil the underside of the food. When broiling, watch food carefully so that it doesn't burn. Most foods will benefit from being turned halfway through the cooking period.

ROAST: Usually a term for meats, but you can "roast" corn or hot dogs on the BBQ when they are cooked at a moderately high heat that allows the juices and fats in the meat to virtually baste itself. Low-fat poultry benefits from human basting every fifteen to twenty minutes. Heat source comes from the bottom of the oven. Quite a few recipes actually call for "French" roasting which means putting the food in a very hot oven, 550°, and then lowering the heat to 350°—375°.

CREMATE: When food is cooked black on the outside. Usually the specialty of uneducated backyard BBQ chefs who think the food should imitate the charcoal or of small children who swear they love black hot dogs and marshmallows to annoy their parents and because they lack the patience to really try to cook anything yet. Really cremated food will not even attract ants.

Hamburger Doesn't Need Help!

Hamburger: Ground beef that comes in several "grades" which really means fat content. The main thing to remember is that the cheaper the cost of beef, the more fat it contains. Some fat, 20% or less, is good because it flavors the meat and keeps it moist while it cooks. Over 20% and the burger will shrink alarmingly!

Basic Burgers

*E

¼ to ⅓ lb. ground beef (per person)
1 hamburger bun per person
salt and pepper to taste
soy sauce, (optional)

Heat a skillet or griddle over medium heat. Put the bun, split side down, buttered or unbuttered, on the grill and brown it. While the bun is browning, form the beef into a patty slightly larger than the bun. Sprinkle each side with salt and pepper or rub each side with a little soy sauce if you like a crispy, salty outside. By the time the bun is ready, the griddle should be perfect for cooking the burger. Cook 3-4 minutes on the first side and turn with a spatula. Juices will start to seep from the patty when it reaches medium rare. While the burger is cooking, you can pile the bun(s) with all the goodies you like on your burger. (If you want a cheese burger, put a slice of your favorite cheese on the patty right after you turn it and put the top bun on.)

Bacon Burgers

*F&E

Follow the directions for Basic Burgers but you can pick your own way to include the bacon. Fry the bacon in the pan after you have browned the bun and cook the burger in the bacon fat. You can also cook the bacon in the microwave (see Pig In). Either set the bacon aside and put it on your burger or break it up into little pieces and mash it into the hamburger as you make the patty.

Surprise Burgers

*E, FFC

You can either fry these in reserved bacon fat or broil them. Try it both ways and see which one works best for you.

⅓ lb. ground beef per person
1 slice of bacon per person
1" x ½" x ¼" piece of cheese (American, cheddar, or Jack)

Make two patties of the beef, sandwich the cheese between the patties, and seal the edges together. Brush with a little soy sauce if you like and fry or broil the burgers until the cheese melts. (Trust me, no one has ever found a way to get two burger patties to seal perfectly, but should you actually achieve the perfectly locked edge, the burger will begin to puff in the center as the molten cheese tries to get out. Transfer the burger to a plate, cover with SECRET SURPRISE SAUCE, and crumble the bacon over the top.

Secret Surprise Sauce

*E, F&C, FFC

This will make enough sauce for one burger but you can increase it for as much as you may need:

1 T. onion, diced
1 t. margarine
⅓ c. ketchup
2 t. Worcestershire sauce
2 t. soy sauce

Sauté the onion in the margarine until it's limp and golden. (Do not brown!) Add the remaining ingredients and simmer on the lowest possible heat while the burger(s) cook.

Sloppy Joes

*E

¼ lb. ground beef (per person)
1 T. onion, diced
1 T. ketchup
1 T. Heinz 57 Sauce
1 T. water
A dash each of garlic salt and chili powder

Spray a small sauce pan or skillet with Pam and break the hamburger in small pieces. Cook the hamburger over medium heat. As the meat begins to cook, add the diced onion and continue cooking, stirring occasionally, until the meat is completely browned and the onion is limp. (Don't worry if the onion isn't wilted yet, it'll get there.) Add all of the other ingredients and simmer, stirring now and then, until it thickens to "sloppy." (Adding another tablespoon of water and cooking the mixture again—makes this even better, blends the flavors, and makes it taste less strongly of hamburger...) Pile this on a bun or pour over a couple of slices of toast.

John Marzetti is one of the primary case studies of why Hamburger Doesn't Need Any Help! You already have everything you need AND it tastes better! All those boxed "helpers" give you is expensive little packets of seasonings and some pasta that you'll have to boil anyway, and that you also probably already have on hand or can substitute noodles or spaghettini for.

John Marzetti

*MC, F-F

You'll want to make this in a batch that will feed 3–4 people so when you have leftovers you can freeze individual servings to nuke later. Zap on Medium High for 3–4 minutes, and you have a well balanced meal—meat, carbohydrates, vegetables, and dairy.

- 1 lb. ground beef
- ½ c. onion, chopped
- 1 t. chili powder
- 1 t. garlic salt
- ¾ c. celery, diced
- 1 (14½ oz.) can tomatoes, diced in their juice

or

- 1 fresh tomato, diced AND 1 small can of tomato juice
- 1½ c. medium egg noodles, cooked, drained, and kept fresh in cool water (see Primary Pasta)
- 2c. cheddar cheese, grated

Brown the beef over medium heat in a large skillet with the onion, chili powder, and garlic salt. When the beef is browned, add the tomatoes and the celery and stir until everything just begins to bubble. Drain the cooked noodles and stir into the meat and veggie goop. PAM an aluminum lasagna pan and pour in the mixture. Top with the cheddar cheese and bake in a 350° oven for 20–30 minutes, or until it is bubbling and the cheese is melted and slightly browned. Let the casserole sit for at least 5 minutes before serving. (Use the time to make a green salad and toast some garlic bread.)

Speedy Spaghetti Sauce

*E

Mother's Disclaimer: This will never be as good as anyone else's mother's spaghetti sauce, which is usually made with a couple of secret ingredients and needs to spend at least 4–8 hours of carefully monitored simmering.

- 1–2 lbs. ground beef
- 1 medium onion, chopped
- 1T. olive oil
- 1c. ketchup
- ¾c. chili sauce (Heinz for this mom)
- 1 (2½ oz.) can tomato paste

1 (5½ oz.) can tomato juice
½ can Campbell's tomato soup
1 small can or jar mushrooms, sliced and undrained (optional)
1½T. Worcestershire sauce

Brown the beef in a large skillet. When it is brown and crumbly, transfer it with a slotted spoon to a large PAMMED sauce pan. To the fat and juices left in the skillet, add the olive oil and the chopped onion. Stir to coat the onions and simmer until they are limp and transparent but not brown. While the onions cook, add the remaining ingredients to the meat and simmer. Add the onions and stir well. Simmer for as long as possible. Like a good stew, a good spaghetti sauce only gets better with long, slow cooking. Stir occasionally while you cook the spaghetti and make some GARLIC BREAD (p. 70). Ladle the sauce generously over the pasta and pass the parmesan.

Save any leftover sauced pasta in one of those little margarine tubs and eat it cold for breakfast. YUMMY! Better than cold pizza any day! If you made too much pasta see Primary Pasta for freezing instructions. Freeze the sauce separately, again in those little tubs. Each tub is the perfect size for one serving. This sauce reheats like a dream—either in a small sauce pan over very low heat or nuked at medium until hot and bubbly. Don't heat the sauce and the pasta together unless you like pink, mushy, yuggy, bland drek.

Lasagna

*TLC, FFC, F-F

Mother's Disclaimer: I may be shot or drummed out of the ranks of cooks in good standing, but lasagna is a time-consuming labor of love: "See how much I REALLY love you? I made LASAGNA!" Excellent frozen lasagna can be found in the 1-,2-, and MOB-size portions. (Stouffer makes a very good product that comes with meat or in a vegetarian model and that can be zapped with okay results.) However, if you are really feeling in need of spending half the day in the kitchen, this is the hamburger sans help for you. Have a deep, aluminum lasagna pan ready, well coated with PAM.

2 boxes lasagna noodles (axiom: 1 box is never enough, but 2 boxes are always too much.)
1 lb. ground beef
1 medium onion, chopped
Garlic powder, fresh garlic, or jarred, crushed garlic to taste
2 (28 oz.) jars of your favorite commercial marinara sauce or other vegetable combination (Paul Newman, Ragu, etc., but if this is really garlicky already, you may want to eliminate the garlic above.)
1 (8 oz.) container ricotta cheese
2 eggs
2T. parsley flakes
1c. provolone cheese, grated
4c. mozzarella cheese, grated
1 (8 oz.) container freshly grated parmesan cheese
Dry (Kraft) parmesan cheese

Cook the lasagna noodles according to the directions on the box with plenty of olive oil and lots of stirring—see Passionate Pasta. Drain and set aside in cool water until assembly time.

Brown beef in a large skillet with the onions (à la Sloppy Joes) until both are done. Add 1 jar of the sauce and the garlic, if you are using it, stir well, and let simmer for 10 minutes. While the meat sauce is simmering, spoon the ricotta into a mixing bowl and beat the 2 eggs and the parsley into the cheese. (Add cooked, chopped, and drained spinach to this mixture and you'll have Lasagna à la Florentine, the usual basis for vegetarian versions.) Spoon a little of the second jar of commercial sauce in the bottom of the pan, tilting it to cover, and you're ready to begin. (I warned you this one takes time!)

Over the thin layer of marinara sauce place a layer of cooked noodles, patted dry, running the long way in the pan. Make sure the curly edges overlap to form a gapless layer. Spoon half of the meat sauce over the noodles, sprinkle with 1 cup of the mozzarella, and sprinkle generously with the Kraft dry parmesan. Add a second layer of noodles over the meat and cheeses, running them the short way this time. Spoon the ricotta/egg mixture in globs on top of the noodles and then spread it out into a nice even layer, but not quite to the outside edges of the pasta. Sprinkle this gooey layer with the fresh parmesan and 1 more cup of the mozzarella. Top this layer with more noodles, running the long way again. Spoon the remaining meat sauce evenly over the pasta and sprinkle with the provolone and 1 more cup mozzarella. You're ALMOST THERE! Now, layer the remaining noodles over the second meat and cheese layer, again running the pasta the short direction. Pour the remaining jar of spaghetti sauce evenly over the pasta and cover this with the last cup of the mozzarella and a generous coating of more dried parmesan. Bake in the center of a 350° oven for 1¼ hours. Remove from oven and let stand at least 10 minutes before cutting into squares to serve. Freeze in individual servings to nuke later.

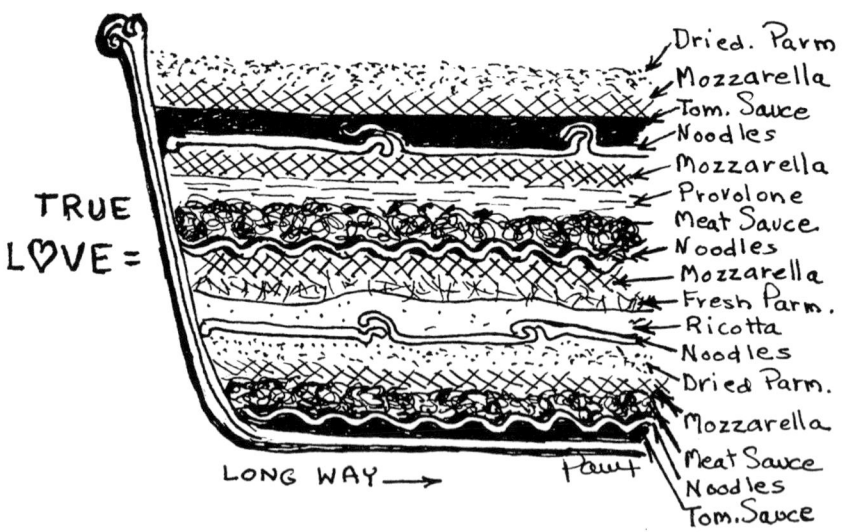

Taco/Tostada Meat

*F&E, F-F

¼–½ lb. ground beef per person
2T. onion, finely diced
2T. green pepper, finely diced, optional
¼t. garlic salt
1t. chili powder
1T. taco sauce or salsa
½ (8 oz.) can Snappy Tom juice cocktail or other Bloody Mary mix
1 (8 oz.) can refried beans
Taco shells or flat corn tostadas (Easy to make your own, just crisp them in hot corn oil, drain, and salt to taste.)

Brown the beef with the onions and green pepper. Sprinkle with the garlic salt and chili powder. Stir in the taco sauce or salsa and the Snappy Tom. Simmer until the filling is almost dry. While the meat is simmering, shred some lettuce and cheddar cheese and dice a fresh tomato. (Warm the beans if you want to use them on your tostada or just to eat on the side!) To make a tostada, spread the tortilla with beans then pile on the meat, lettuce, cheese, tomato, and extra sauce or salsa. For a taco, stuff the shell with the meat and then the fresh vegetables and cheese as above.

Use this same recipe for meat, sprinkle it liberally over warm tortilla chips and smother with microzapped jalapeña-cheese sauce for **Super Nachos**. For an appetizer, PAM a Pyrex baking dish. Layer the beans, meat, and cheese and bake at 325º till the cheese melts, top with veggies, and scoop with chips.

Mega Meatballs

*MC, FFC, F-F

SAUCY ITALIAN—Great for meatball sandwiches or over pasta. Freeze any leftover meatballs in their sauce, and they're even better the second time around.

¼–⅓ lb. ground beef
2T. onion, finely diced
½t. garlic salt
½t. dried Italian herbs or basil

Mix all of the ingredients together with your clean hands, (Hey! I AM a mother.) and form into medium-sized balls, about 4 from ¼ lb. of meat. Brown them in a skillet in a little olive oil, then remove them to a small plate. Add the following to the pan with the oil and brown bits:

1 slice of onion cut in half
¼ green pepper cut into strips

Lower the heat and sauté the vegetables until tender, stirring. Add:

½c. spaghetti sauce, marinara, or your favorite commercial tomato/herb sauce

Return the meatballs to the sauced vegetables and simmer for 10 minutes more.

BBQ BEAUTIES—This makes a lot of meatballs if you use the MEATLOAF/SALISBURY STEAK recipe, but they freeze well and make great nibblers. Just shape the meatballs, brown in a little vegetable oil, and simmer in your favorite BBQ sauce.

SIMPLY SWEDISH—This recipe makes 2 servings as a main course with noodles or enough appetizers for 4–5. These are a classic hot dish for a party buffet.

¼ lb. ground beef

¼ lb. ground pork

¼ lb. ground veal, chicken, or turkey

1 slice white bread soaked in 2T. milk

2 sardines, smashed, or 1t. anchovy paste

2T. onion, finely diced and sautéed in a little margarine or oil until golden

2 eggs, beaten

1T. parsley flakes

2t. lemon juice

Olive oil

1 can consommé

½ soup can water

1 can Campbell's cream of mushroom soup

1t. dried dill weed

Combine the first 10 ingredients in a bowl and mash them together with your hands until completely mixed. Form into small (1 T.) balls. (They will be gooey.) in a large skillet brown the meatballs over medium heat in a little olive oil. Cook them in batches without crowding them so that you can roll them around easily. Remove the browned meatballs to a large bowl with a slotted spoon. Turn off the burner.

Bring the consommé and water to a gentle boil and add the meatballs. Turn the heat down and simmer the meatballs for 15 minutes. While the meatballs are simmering, make the sauce.

Add the mushroom soup to the skillet you used to brown the meatballs, scraping up the little brown pieces left in the pan as you stir in the dill weed. It will be very thick, but don't worry. When the meatballs are done, drain off 1 soup can of the broth and add it to the dilled soup. Bring the sauce to a simmer to coat them evenly. Serve immediately with a green salad or put in a warming pot as an hors d'oeuvre. Provide the fuzzy toothpicks and you'll really "Impress the Guests!"

Meatloaf/Salisbury Steak

*MC, F-F

One of the few foods that has acquired a fancy name for a smaller portion. Bottom line, a Salisbury Steak is really just an individual meatloaf, usually covered in a brown or mushroom sauce instead of a tomato or ketchup-based sauce. Big deal! ¼ lb. ground beef serves 1 person, so make one small meatloaf for two people, or 2 Salisbury steaks and freeze one, after it is cooked, to zap later.

½ lb. ground beef
1 egg
2T. ketchup
2T. Heinz 57 sauce
Dash of garlic powder
1T. parsley flakes
8 Ritz crackers, crumbled

PAM an aluminum loaf pan or square pan and set it aside. Using your hands, mix all of the ingredients together well in a large mixing bowl. It will be a little bit slippery (but don't worry about that). Shape it into a solid loaf and plop it into the loaf pan. Make a long indentation down the center of the loaf and pour

1 (5½ oz.) can tomato juice

over the loaf. Then pour a line of ketchup down the indentation. Bake at 350° for 45 minutes to 1 hour or until clear juices run out of the top of the center of the loaf. Let stand at least 10 minutes before slicing and serving.

To turn this into Salisbury steaks, make two mini-loaves and place them slightly apart in a PAMMED baking pan. Brush the tops with a little soy sauce and roast in a 375° oven for 25–30 minutes.

Either meatloaf or its "little brothers" can be fancied-up. Try stuffing either one with a block of cheddar cheese. For an Italian touch, add a block of mozzarella and heat some of your favorite pasta sauce to spoon over them before serving. Try spinach and bacon or stuffing mix. Use your imagination, and meatloaf could become a real dining experience!

Foolproof Fowl

Sesame Chicken

*F & E, FFC

This recipe serves two, but it freezes well, so if you make a larger amount you can store the leftovers in Ziplock baggies for CHICKEN SALADS or CHICKEN TACOS.

- 1 package chicken tenders
- 2 T. soy sauce
- 2 slices onion, separated into rings
- 1 T. sesame oil
- 2 T. sunflower oil
- 1 T. sesame seeds

Separate the chicken tenders and layer them in a glass bowl. Toss them with the soy sauce to coat and set aside. Combine the two oils in a medium or large skillet and sauté the onions over low heat until they are limp but not brown. Remove the onions with a slotted spoon and set them aside. Turn the heat up to medium and add the chicken in a single layer. When the bottoms start to brown and the meat begins to change from pink to white, sprinkle with the sesame seeds and turn each tender over with tongs. Cook another 2–3 minutes and stir in the onions. Heat 1 more minute and serve with rice. (See Independent Study in Starches)

Mimosa BBQ Chicken

"GRAND CHAMPION RECIPE DEL MAR BBQ CONTEST"

*E, FFC

- 6–12 fryer chicken pieces (thighs and drum sticks recommended)
- 1 (8 oz.) bottle Wishbone Deluxe French Dressing
- 1 (8 oz.) bottle Wishbone Deluxe Italian Dressing
- 1 c. fresh orange juice
- 2t. liquid smoke
- 1 gallon-sized Ziplock bag

(You can call any recipe that uses oranges or orange juice "Mimosa" whatever.)

Combine the dressings, orange juice, and liquid smoke in a bowl and whisk together. Dip each piece of chicken in the marinade and drop them in the Ziplock bag. After all the pieces are dipped, pour the remaining marinade over the chicken and seal the bag. Toss in the icebox and let it sit for at least 2 hours or overnight. Cook over medium coals, basting with the marinade and turning often. Great hot or cold and okay to reheat in the microwave. Make plenty because the neighbors may drop in when they smell this cooking!

Chicken, Plain Good

*E, FFC

1 whole chicken breast, boned, skinned, and cut into halves
2 T. flour
salt and pepper to taste
1 T. margarine or butter
1 T. sunflower oil
1 T. parsley flakes
2 T. margarine or butter
2 t. crushed garlic, optional
1 T. lemon juice, optional
2 t. capers, optional

Sprinkle the flour on a medium-sized plate and season with salt and pepper. Heat the oil and 1 T. of margarine in a medium skillet over medium heat until it just begins to color. Dredge the chicken breasts in the flour and place, cut side down, in the skillet. Sauté for 3 minutes. Turn and cook an additional 3 minutes on the second side. Remove to warm plates and immediately add the 2 T. margarine and parsley (as well as garlic, lemon juice, and capers if you wish), stirring till it browns slightly. Pour the sauce over the chicken and serve immediately. Most markets won't sell you just half a chicken breast, so cook both halves and use the second half as per SESAME CHICKEN leftovers.

(This recipe is also perfect for veal, if you can afford this luxury meat, when you really want to impress someone special!)

Fried Chicken

*F & E

FORGET IT! You can buy this at one of the national chicken chains for less cost and effort than doing it at home. By the time you want to try this one, you should be good enough in the kitchen to have invested in a bigger cook book like the *Joy of Cooking*, the second book you should add to your growing kitchen library. (Ask your Mom for that one as a Christmas present and see her reaction!)

Chicken Salad

*F & E, FFC

6-7 chicken tenders or 1 half chicken breast, cooked and diced
⅓ c. mayonnaise
1 t. lime (or lemon) juice
2 t. onion, minced or finely diced
¼ c. celery, diced
1 T. cashews, chopped or crushed, optional

Combine the mayonnaise, juice, onion, celery, and salt and pepper (to taste). Stir in the diced chicken. Spoon onto a lettuce leaf and sprinkle with the cashews. Very refreshing and perfect with fruit and a warm roll.

Oriental Chicken Salad

*E, FFC

6-7 chicken tenders or half a chicken breast, cooked and diced
1 c. head lettuce, broken into bite-size pieces
1 green onion, thinly sliced
¼ c. green pepper, diced
6–8 canned water chestnuts, sliced (buy the whole variety so that you can use the leftovers for NUKED CHINESE NIBBLERS.)
½ c. La Choy Chow Mein Noodles

DRESSING:
2 T. olive oil
1 T. sesame oil
1 T. red wine vinegar or rice vinegar
¼ t. sugar
1 T. soy sauce
2 t. dried chives
2 t. sesame seeds

Arrange all of the salad ingredients except the noodles in a chilled bowl. Combine all of the dressing ingredients in a small jar and shake well. Pour over the salad and top with the noodles. Toss well.

Chicken Tacos

*E

6–7 chicken tenders or half chicken breast, cooked and shredded
2 slices onion, separated into rings
¼ green pepper, cut into strips
1 T. corn oil
1 (8 oz.) can Snappy Tom

Sauté the onions and peppers in the oil over medium heat until limp. Stir in the Snappy Tom and the shredded chicken and simmer till almost no liquid remains. (Don't try to boil this down at 90 miles an hour! Your goal is to flavor the chicken, not turn it into rubber bands.) Pile the meat and vegetables into 2 taco shells and add shredded lettuce, grated cheese, diced tomatoes, and sauce or salsa.

TACO a la GOODYEAR

A Fowl By-Product

THE EGG (*L'OEUF* in French, probably based on the sound the poor hen makes "*Oeuf! Oeuf! Mon Dieu*, another one of those darn baby carriers!") This little bundle of protein and protoplasm does contain cholesterol, but you need to remember that if you save your whites—freeze them in a plastic bowl or one-by-one in an ice cube tray and then pop them into a Ziplock bag to thaw when you need them— you can decrease the cholesterol. Add an extra egg white to any egg recipe that calls for beaten eggs, and you'll cut the evil in half and get a fluffier result.

Boiled Eggs

*F & E

Boil water (enough to cover the eggs) in a sauce pan. Add a little vinegar to the water in case the shock of the hot water on the poor cold egg causes it to crack up. The vinegar will keep the egg's white from spewing into the water creating a very watery Egg Drop Soup. (An egg that's spilled its guts is an ugly sight, especially first thing in the morning when most people feel they need to cook an egg.) Gently lower the egg into the water, and when the water returns to a boil start timing.

2 minutes, very soft
3 minutes, soft
4 minutes, almost firm white, runny yolk
5 minutes, firm white, soft yolk

Crack open immediately (using napkins or hot pads) because as long as the egg is in the shell, it will continue to cook.

Hard-Boiled Eggs

*E

Place eggs in a sauce pan just large enough to hold the number you want. Cover them with cold water. Add I T. vinegar and bring to a boil over MEDIUM heat. Once the water reaches a rolling boil, cook the eggs for 10 minutes. Longer won't hurt, but don't let the water boil away!! The easiest way to peel hard-boiled eggs is to put the whole pan in the sink under cool running water. Add 6 ice cubes, and when the water is cool enough to put your hands in, remove the eggs one at a time. Break the shell completely and peel the egg under the stream of cool water. The cold shock causes the shell to separate from the hot egg, and the shell should come off easily. Let the peeled eggs cool on the counter, then bag them and put them in the icebox unless you are going to use them immediately. If you are boiling the eggs to make DEVILED EGGS, you will want to slice them in half while they are still hot so that the yolks melt the butter. The butter makes the egg yolk filling firm as it cools. (So who said boiling eggs was easy? I've just written a page on this rather mundane subject, so let's move on!)

Fried Eggs

*F & E

Best handled one or two at a time because eggs that have come out of their shells can be fussy and need personalized attention, not to be confused with coddling. (A coddled egg is cooked inside a special little lidded pot in boiling water. From this we get the verb to handle with care. This method is really designed to coddle the eater who doesn't want to contend with a boiling hot egg, still in its shell, before they've finished their morning paper.) If you are the cautious type, break the egg(s) into a bowl first and then slip them into the skillet when the butter or margarine is melted over medium heat. If you like your eggs "sunny side" up, you may want to cook the yolk a little more by tilting the pan, collecting the hot butter in a spoon and basting the yolk. If you like the yolk runny just wait till the white is done and slip, or pry, them out of the skillet with a spatula and onto your plate. "Over easy" means just that. You have to get your spatula completely under the egg, especially under the yolk, and flip it over so that the yolk doesn't break. (Easy for me say! This mom is a firm believer in basting eggs.)

Poached Eggs

*MC

This method cooks eggs outside of their shells either over or in simmering water. To poach eggs in water takes a talent that I have yet to master, so if your mother poaches eggs this way get HER to show you how. I believe in the poacher which is a pan that holds water, a metal plate with holes that hold little poaching cups, and a lid. (Single egg poachers usually have just the little cup that sits over the water.) Poachers come in all sizes from one-egg to twelve-cup professional restaurant size. Put water in the pan, just to below the cup bottoms, and bring it to a simmer over medium heat. PAM the cup and put a dab of butter or margarine in it. Place the cup over the water and when the butter melts, crack an egg into it. Put the lid on and check it in 5 minutes. This method gently steams the egg. Take the lid off and jiggle the pan by the handle. The white should be opaque, but the yolk should still be wobbly. Take the cup off the water and turn it over your toast or English muffin bottom. It should plop right out.

Scrambled Et Al

*MC

The ultimate cosmopolitan egg. Put a bit of butter, margarine, or oil in a skillet and heat it till it becomes fragrant, then let the world inspire you!

1, 2, or 3 eggs
Salt and pepper to taste
Dash of Tabasco, optional
Dash of Worcestershire sauce, optional

Crack the egg(s) into a bowl, add the other ingredients, and beat well with a fork. (Scramble them.) Pour the eggs into the heated skillet and stir them gently till they are as hard, or as soft, as you like them.

Now the et al:

Prepared as above they are just plain old scrambled eggs, BUT...

A. Stir them just a little bit with the scrambling fork and toss any of the following on top. Let the topping(s) meld or melt, then just fold the eggs over while they are still a little soft and you have the **OMELET** avec:

Fresh Herbs	Bacon	Ham
Cooked Veggies	Cheese	Raw Veggies
Green Ortega Chilies	Fruits	Caviar
Cooked Sausage	Jam	The Kitchen Sink!

B. Pour the beaten eggs in the skillet, but don't stir them, just lift a corner of the eggs and let the slime run underneath. Sprinkle the surface with grated cheese, cheddar or Jack or both. Add some diced mild chilies and a little salsa. Fold it over. It may crack a little because the bottom is crisp. Add a little extra salsa on top and you have created—**OLÉ SPANISH OMELET!**

C. Mix any goodies you want into the eggs and pour them into the hot oil.(You might try onion, green peppers, ham, pepperoni, parmesan, diced fried potatoes, black olives, anchovies, mozzarella—sound like a pizza...read on!) Cook the eggs till brown on the bottom then flip the whole thing over like a giant pancake. Brown on the second side and slide onto a large plate. Cut into wedges and serve it with warm pasta sauce. You've just created the Italian "omelet" known as a **FRITTATA**.

D. Sauté diced onion, green pepper, and ham in the butter. Pour the eggs over these and stir them all together. If you keep stirring you have a DENVER SCRAMBLE. If you stir it just a little with the fork and fold it in half, with or without a little cheese, you have a **DENVER OMELET**.

E. Eggs for dinner? This is a classic Chinese side dish. Scramble the eggs with a dash or two of soy sauce. Optional veggies to add include any of the following:

Bean Sprouts	Sliced Mushrooms	Celery
Onion	Green Onion	Sliced Water Chestnuts

Use vegetable oil with 1t. of sesame oil and fry the egg two tablespoons at a time. (Here is a great place to add a saved egg white.) When the egg "cake" has puffed up and browned on the first side, flip it over and brown the other side. Sprinkle generously with salt and enjoy **EGG FOO YUNG!!**

Egg Salad

*F & E

For one sandwich:
- 1 hard boiled egg, chopped
- 2 T. mayonnaise
- 1 dash Tabasco
- Salt and pepper to taste
- 1 t. onion, minced, optional
- 1 T. celery, diced, optional
- 1 T. green pepper, diced, optional
- 4 stuffed olives, sliced, optional
- 2 slices bacon, crisply zapped, optional
- 1 small squirt of mustard, optional

Mix the egg, mayonnaise, and seasonings together. Add any, or all, of the other ingredients and mix well. (Save the bacon and put it on top.) Smear on a slice of bread and cover with a second slice.

Deviled Eggs

*E, F&C

You'll always need to make a few more of these than you think you'll need because EVERYONE seems to love these, no matter what you put in them! (AXIOM: When you go to a Pot Luck, the deviled eggs will always be gone before you can find out what they tasted like... and everyone is raving about how good they were!) Try the plain, basic, but always good variety.

- 2 hot hard boiled eggs
- 1 T. butter (no substitutions here!)
- 1 T. mayonnaise
- 1 t. pickle relish (if you like them sweet)
- 1 small squirt mustard (if you like them tart)
- Pinch of curry powder (if you like them spicy)

Slice the hot eggs in half (lengthwise) and pop the hot yolks into a small bowl or Pyrex custard cup with the butter. Mash the egg yolks and butter together well with a fork and add the other ingredients, combining well until smooth. Pile the egg yolk mixture into the egg white cavities. Sprinkle with a little paprika or some parsley flakes for color and place on a plate. Chill, covered, in the icebox until ready to serve. Okay for a fill-in "Impress the Guest" but even better at a BBQ, casual party, lunch, or picnic.

The Anatomy of
the Rib

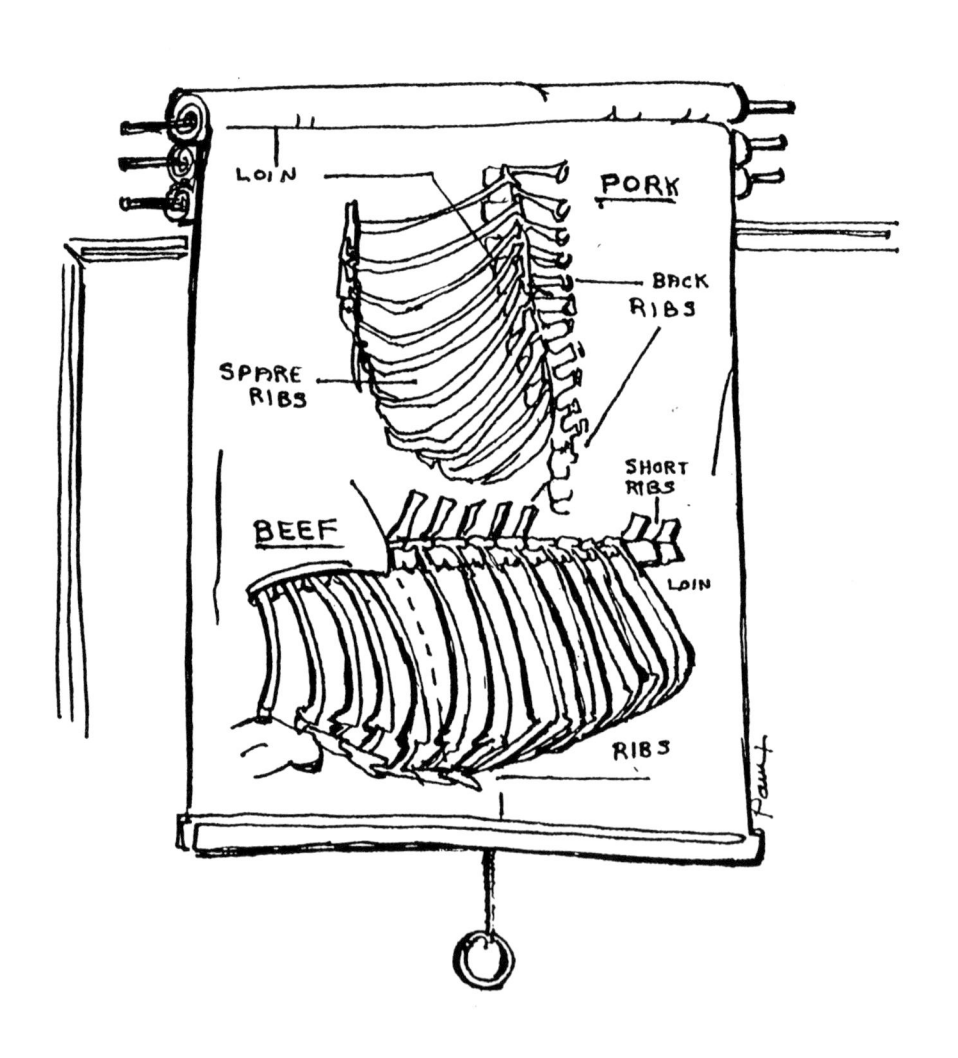

There are three basic types of ribs

BEEF—Big, juicy, look great, but the proportion of meat to bone is not very economical. On the plus side, big beef ribs are relatively fast and easy to cook. Beef short ribs tend to be fatty and take longer to cook, but are tender.

PORK—Two styles you might like to try are the baby back ribs and the country cut. Both need long, slow cooking because pork needs to be well done...unless you like the idea of little tiny worms wending their ways through your muscles, a.k.a. TRICHINOSIS

LAMB—Usually called "riblets," they are easy to cook and an inexpensive answer to a craving for this more expensive meat. These make good "Impress the Guest" bites—not much meat but very tender.

Oven BBQ Guacho Beef Ribs
*MC, FFC

Start with the two sauces. Mix each in its own bowl and then set them aside till you need them.

Sauce 1:
- **1 c. Heinz chili sauce**
- **2 t. chili powder**
- **2 t. liquid smoke**
- **Dash of garlic powder to taste**

Sauce 2:
- **1 c. Heinz 57 sauce**
- **¼ c. water**
- **1 t. liquid smoke**
- **2—3 large beef ribs per person**

Hint: Cook at least six and use the leftovers for BBQ beef sandwiches.

PAM a large, square aluminum roaster. Place the ribs in it, meaty side down. Combine ¼ c. of each sauce in a third bowl. Spoon and spread half of this combined sauce over the bony sides of the ribs. Roast uncovered in the middle of a 350° oven for 15 minutes. Turn the ribs over with tongs and cover the meaty side with the remaining combined sauce. Roast another 10 minutes for rare, longer if you prefer medium to well done.

To be "fancy" you can serve the ribs Guacho Style. Place 2–3 ribs on their sides on each plate. Spoon Sauce 1 over the top halves of the ribs and Sauce 2 over the bottom halves to present a nice color contrast. (NOTE: This is the fancy way, but since the sauces will get all mixed up as you eat the ribs anyway, this recipe is just as good when you mix the two sauces to start with!)

BBQ Short Ribs

*MC

Short ribs have more meat, more fat, and need a longer cooking time because they are a tougher, therefore cheaper cut of beef. Because this rib cooks slowly with onion slices, you can save the cooked onions and add them to any leftover meat for a really luscious BBQ sandwich! If you want to dress up these ribs, you can serve them with the sauces separated as above.

- 1–2 lbs. Beef short ribs
- 1 large onion, thinly sliced
- Sauces 1 and 2, mixed together
- Garlic salt to taste

PAM an aluminum roasting pan. (This is a real pitch dish—it's very messy!) Spread ¼ c. of the sauce evenly over the bottom of the pan. Sprinkle the ribs with garlic salt to taste. Layer ½ of the onion rings over the sauce then add the ribs on their edges. Spread another ¼ c. of the sauce over the ribs and cover with the remaining onion rings. Cover with aluminum foil, sealing tightly around the edges, and bake in the middle of a 325° oven for 2 hours.

Remove the foil carefully because there will be lots of steam. Put the onions in a bowl if you want to save them. Remove the ribs to a plate. Scoop out the remaining onions with a slotted spoon if you want to use them. The liquid will be very greasy. Pour off the liquid in the pan and dispose of it in the trash after it cools because you won't want this clogging up your pipes! Return the ribs to the pan and cover with the remaining sauce—save ½ c. if you plan on having leftovers for sandwiches—and roast uncovered at 375° for 15-20 minutes.

Heavenly "Stinky" Pork Ribs
(Basic Recipe)

*MC, TLC
- 2–4 lbs. baby back pork ribs (You'll want leftovers!)
- 3 cans beer
- 6 limes
- 1 T. liquid smoke
- Garlic salt

Make a small cut in the meaty part between each rib, top and bottom, about ½ inch long, then separate them into 2-3 rib groups. Sprinkle the ribs liberally with garlic salt. Pour the beer into a large pot with a tightly fitting lid. Add 3 beer cans of water, the juice of the limes, and the liquid smoke. Stir. Add the ribs to the liquid and add water, if necessary, to cover. Put on the lid and simmer on low heat for 3 hours. Remove the pot from the heat and allow it to cool. At this point the ribs are ready to use immediately, or store them in Ziplock bags to wait in the icebox, or freeze them for future use.

BBQ:

Make a recipe of Guacho Sauce. PAM an aluminum roasting pan. Dip the rib clusters into the sauce and place them in the pan, meaty side up. Because the ribs are already cooked, you'll only reheat them to glaze them with the sauce. Roast them in a 350° oven for 15 minutes. Warm a little of the extra sauce and serve it on the side if you want more. These should be the most tender, most fall-apart ribs you've ever tasted.

CHINESE SWEET AND SOUR RIBS:

Cook ribs by the basic recipe. Experiment with some of the many varieties of sweet and sour sauces available in the Oriental food section of the market until you find one you really like. Dip the rib clusters in the sauce to coat. (You may want to thin the sauce with a little water as some of them are very thick!) Place the ribs, meaty side up, in a PAMMED roasting pan and roast them in the middle of a 350° oven for 10 minutes. Sprinkle the ribs generously with sesame seeds and roast for 5 minutes longer to crisp the seeds. Serve as an appetizer, "Impress the Guests," or with a Chinese dinner.

Lamb Riblets

*MC, FFC
8-10 lamb riblets (per person for a meal)
5-6 lamb riblets (per person for an appetizer)
1 (6 oz.) can pineapple juice
2 sprigs fresh mint or 1 T. mint flakes
1 T. rosemary, crushed
2 cloves garlic, cut in slivers

Cut the ribs into 2-3 rib clusters. Place them in a Ziplock bag with extra room. Add all of the other ingredients, close tightly, test the seal, and then shake well to combine. Let the ribs marinate overnight in the icebox. Drain the ribs, saving the marinade. You can either BBQ these over medium coals* or roast them in a 350° oven for 20 minutes. Either way you will want to baste them every 5 minutes with the marinade.

*When coals are uniformly gray, place your hand about 6 inches above them and start counting, slowly. If you can count to 5 or 6 before you have to remove your hand, the coals will be at approximately 350°. Do not use this method if you enjoy pain.

Axiom Numero Uno

Never, NEVER NEVER! tell anyone what is actually in what they are eating. You will have at least a 50% chance of seeing what you have offered in love and friendship remain uneaten on the plate for the rest of the meal. Try "Oh, really? Do you like it? I just sort of threw it together." Or "Oh, what do you think the 'green things' are? I had three 'green things' on my shopping list. What do you like that's green? Humm, yes! That must be what it is—finely diced, of course." Even such harmless vegetables as parsley or chives can be imagined to be poison to some people, so cook's amnesia is often kinder for all concerned.

Cook's Prerogative

This is *the* phrase that allows you, the cook, to taste what you are cooking. It also allows you to sample and keep one or two choice nibblers for yourself, like sampling just a little of the steak as you carve or popping that extra olive in your mouth. It is also the main cause of overweight cooks.

Pig In!

Pork, in all its varied forms, has one MAJOR RULE OF COOKING. It must be thoroughly cooked. Even though the Jewish mother of 1,000 B.C.E. had never heard of trichinosis, she followed Kosher laws and never cooked pork for her family. Like many Orthodox prohibitions, the dietary laws were based on solid evidence of what foods could kill people. Improperly cooked pork was one of these, so it was better not to take any chances. Microwaving on Medium is now the best available way to cook pork so that it is moist but safe. Medium cooking with a cover of Saran Wrap allows the meat to cook evenly and still remain moist. Slow roasting, frying, and stewing will also get the job done.

Basic Bacon

*MC

PAM a large skillet or griddle and put the desired number of bacon strips in or on it. Turn the heat up to Medium. When the fat in the bacon starts to sizzle, your work begins. There are two parts to perfect bacon—tending and turning.

Bacon is not a food you want to walk away from and leave on the heat—unless you really want to start a fire. When the bacon starts to become translucent turn each strip over, top to bottom. As the closest ends begin to turn whitish-brown, turn the strips sideways. When the bacon starts to foam and bubble through each strip, turn it end over end again. When each strip is covered with fine bubbles, it is done. Remove each strip as it finishes to a double layer of paper towels and blot with another towel.

This tending and turning guarantees that each side and end of each bacon strip gets the cooking time it needs to become a crisp, uniformly cooked, elongated little piece of heaven on earth!

Note: This time-honored way of cooking is prenuke and produces a lot of grease. Nuking the piglet is much healthier, but bacon grease is great for frying hamburgers and absolutely essential for a good hot bacon dressing or German potato salad. (As I've said before, buy the *Joy of Cooking*.)

Nuked Bacon

*E, M

This bacon needs no turning or tending because the microwaves zip right through it. It is absolutely the best reason for the invention of the microwave oven!!! It is as grease-free as possible, easy to do, easy to clean up, and with the best, most uniform results!

NOTE: This is fast but not foolproof.

- 1 paper plate (thick) or 2–3 cheapies.
- 2 squares of paper towels on top of each other
- 1–4 strips of bacon
- 1 square of paper towel to cover
- 1 square of paper towel to blot

Layer as listed except for the last piece of toweling. For each piece of bacon allow 1 minute of zap time on High. So for 1 piece, zap for 30 seconds, give the plate a half turn, and zap for 30 seconds more. For 2 pieces zap for 1 minute, give the plate a half turn, and zap for 1 minute more, etc. If you have to cook a huge batch, you can even put layers of bacon on top of each other, but watch the timing! NOTE: When it stops sizzling and popping, it is done. The more pieces you are cooking, the less time is sometimes required, depending upon the thickness and the content of the bacon. You still have to pay attention, albeit for a shorter period of time.

When the bacon is done:
1. Take the plate out of the oven.
2. Wipe any grease or moisture off the bottom of the oven.
3. Lift the top towel off the bacon.
4. Blot the bacon with the dry towel.
5. Remove the bacon to your plate and let it sit for about a minute to finish crisping up.

Pork Chops
*MC

This prosaic little rib and meat main course can be tasteless, dry, and an eating trial…or a delicate treat. Whether you like them PLAIN with a little applesauce on the side or smothered in gravy or sauce, the key to good swine is moisture!

PLAIN:

1 pork chop (per person), ½ to 1½ inches thick
Garlic salt to taste
¼ t. rosemary, crushed, optional

MICROWAVE:

Place chop(s) on a microwave-safe plate and cover with plastic wrap. Zap on Medium 1 minute per ½ inch, give the plate a half turn, and cook 1 minute more per ½ inch. The meat will be moist and tender but not browned. (Tip: Let the chop stand, uncovered, for one or two minutes to let the meat stop "bubbling internally" before cutting.)

SKILLET:

PAM a skillet and add the prepared chop(s). Turn up the heat to Medium-high and brown on the first side. Turn over and reduce the heat to Medium. When juices begin to run clear, or after 5–7 minutes, the chop should be done. These will be nicely browned but a little drier.

BAKED:

PAM an aluminum pan. Preheat the oven to 325°. Put the prepared chop(s) in the pan and pop in the oven. Cook 10 minutes on each side. Cut into the chop at the thickest part AND next to the bone at the T on the large side. If there is any pink, or if the juices look bloody to pink, continue cooking until they run clear. Moister than fried but a little more effort.

Mother's Side Tip: If you want to add a little something to that "plain old applesauce on the side," spice it up with just a small dab of prepared horseradish. Add a drop of red food coloring for a "special occasion." Even people who never touch horseradish seem to like this. "Uuhmm! What did you add to the applesauce?" You can just smile and say, "Oh, just a little secret my mother taught me." Never admit what the "secret" ingredient is because 50% of the world will swear they are allergic to it, 25% will hate it, and the other 25% are purists: "How could you put good horseradish in applesauce!"

Smothered Pork Chops

*MC

Since the base word for smothered is mother, it seems to follow that each and every one has her own "special" recipe, but this is a basic recipe.

> 4 ½–1 inch thick pork chops
>
> 1 can of Campbell's cream of just about anything soup—mushroom, celery, broccoli, vegetable, etc.
>
> 1 T. dried herb, crushed (try sage, rosemary, basil, or chives…experiment!)

PAM a skillet well and brown the chops on both sides over High heat. Combine the soup, herbs, and a little milk or water to make a thick sauce (the pork chop juices will dilute it a little more as they cook). PAM an aluminum baking pan that is just large enough to hold the chops in one layer and spoon a little of the sauce in the bottom. Add the chops and cover with the rest of the sauce. Bake in a 350° oven, uncovered, for 1 hour. Remove the chops to serving plates and stir the sauce to incorporate the pork juices. Divide the sauce equally over the chops. This freezes well and zaps back with excellent results on Medium power.

Ham Slice

*M, F & E

This can be an expensive piece of meat, but if you think a good, whole ham for $50 is out of sight, just stop and figure out what you are paying for those thin little slices pressed and packaged in with the other deli meats. OUCH! The solution to this budget-buster is to buy a ham slice. One slice will serve 4 people nicely with a little left over for sandwich slices, diced to use in scrambled eggs or minced for HAM SALAD. You can also freeze remainders and rezap them to perfection.

> 1 ham slice (Farmer John has a good product.)
>
> 4 slices pineapple, optional
>
> 4 t. brown sugar, optional
>
> maraschino cherries, optional

Place the ham slice on a microwave-safe plate and zap at Medium power for 1 minute. Give the plate a half turn and zap 1 minute more. Let stand 1 minute and serve.

To make this fit for a party, just cover it with the pineapple slices. Sprinkle each slice with 1 t. of the brown sugar and plop a cherry in the center. Add ½ minute to both of the cooking times given above.

Ham Salad
(Real and Imitation)

*E

REAL HAM SALAD may be made to taste—sweet, sour, bland, or spicy—but IMITATION has to be sweet or it just doesn't work.

REAL HAM SALAD:

For one sandwich:

- ¼ **c. ham, minced**
- **1 T. celery, finely diced**
- **1-2 T. mayonnaise (Best Foods=bland))**
- **or**
- **1-2 T. salad dressing (Miracle Whip=sweet)**
- **1 t. onion, minced**
- **1 t. mustard, (optional—sour or spicy, depending upon the type you use)**
- **2 t. sweet pickle relish (optional—sweet)**
- **3 dill pickle slices, diced (optional—sour)**
- **4 stuffed olives, diced (optional—salty and sour)**

Combine the ingredients of your choice and let the salad rest in the icebox for an hour or more, allowing the flavors to blend.

IMITATION HAM SALAD:

Not exactly a "classified" secret recipe but strange enough that a lot of people wouldn't even consider the possible ingredients. For one sandwich:

- **1 hot dog, ground through a meat grinder, shredded through a super shooter or vegetable grater and then chopped, or minced as finely as possible.**
- **1 T. celery, finely diced**
- **2 T. Miracle Whip (and only Miracle Whip)**
- **1 t. onion, finely diced**
- **1 T. sweet pickle relish**
- **Squirt of French's mustard, optional but good**

Stir all of the ingredients together well. If it seems a little dry, add more Miracle Whip till it is the way you like it. That hot dog will soak up a lot! Store, covered, in the icebox for at least 12 hours or this recipe doesn't work. It is the "aging process" that gets rid of the hot dog taste and turns it into "ham."

Dad's Hot Dog Special
*F & E

As dictated to this writer by her beloved husband. Makes one sandwich:

2 slices of squishy white bread, lightly toasted

2 hot dogs, split and "grilled" in a PAMMED skillet over Medium-high heat (Cook cut side down first.)

Mustard, optional, Dad, being the creator of this gastronomic treat, and therefore a purist, gives mustard three "thumbs down!", but Mom likes it with mustard.

Spread both pieces of toast generously with the Miracle Whip. Pick your bottom slice and lay the onion on it and then the hot dogs. (Mom puts her mustard on top of the dogs.) On top of the top slice of toast add the pickle slices, tomato slices, (more Miracle Whip if you like it really drippy/gooey) and the lettuce leaf. Join the two halves and chow down with plenty of paper napkins or paper towels and an order of Fritos.

Note: Even the nastiest, smelliest, strongest onion can be tamed with just a little forethought and patience. If you allow sliced, diced, or chopped onion a little time to breathe before you use it raw, it will tone down and become civilized. Just cut what you want and let it sit on the cutting board for half an hour or more to allow the acidic fumes to evaporate, making the onion a mellow vegetable with plenty of flavor but not too much bite.

Oven BBQ Hot Dogs
*E, F-F

Tip: Make a whole batch of these because:

A. They freeze and reheat well in the oven.

B. They freeze and rezap well.

C. The frozen leftovers can be cut into small chunks, returned to the sauce, and reheated for "Impress the Guests."

D. Every man, woman, and child who has ever eaten these LOVES THEM!

1 package hot dogs (10–12), pierced or spiral cut to absorb the sauce flavor

BBQ SAUCE:

½ c. onion, diced

1 T. brown sugar

2 T. lemon juice

½ c. ketchup

1 t. French's mustard

¼ c. water

¼ c. celery, diced

1 T. margarine

Preheat the oven to 350°. Brown the onion in the margarine over Medium heat then add all of the other ingredients except the hot dogs. Stir to combine well and lower the heat. Simmer the sauce over Low heat for 30 minutes. PAM a shallow aluminum pan, just large enough to hold all of the dogs and spoon a little of the sauce in the bottom to cover. Arrange the hot dogs over the sauce and cover with the rest of the sauce. Bake uncovered for 30 minutes.

Pigs in a Blanket

*F & E, M
1–2 hot dog(s) per person
1 slice bacon per dog
Long thin slices of cheddar cheese, optional

Half-cook the bacon in the microwave so that it is limp. If you are in a cheesy mood, slit the hot dog the long way, but not quite all the way through. Stuff the cheese into the slit. Wrap the bacon around the dog, securing it at each end with a tooth pick. Put two paper towels on a paper plate and place the dogs on it, cheese side up. Zap the pigs on high for the rest of the time needed to cook the bacon.

Ichthyology

Gutting the Sucker

Show no mercy. Hack off the head. Firmly slit the fish from stem to stern. Pull all of the innards out with your hand under running water. Holding the fish by the tail, gently scrape off the scales from each side. It is now ready for the pan if you don't mind the battle of the bones. If you prefer a slightly better chance of not choking to death on your dinner, now is a good time to fillet the fish. Slit the fish along the back—slightly down from the dorsal (back) fin to the tail and then down from the top of the tail. Using the knife, gently separate the fish from its skeleton till you have a fillet. Flip the fish over and fillet the other side. There is no need to skin a fish—that's about as time consuming and necessary as peeling a grape! Your roommates may appreciate you more if you clean the fish on old newspaper and throw the inedibles away in an outside trash can with a lid. Dead fish STINK!

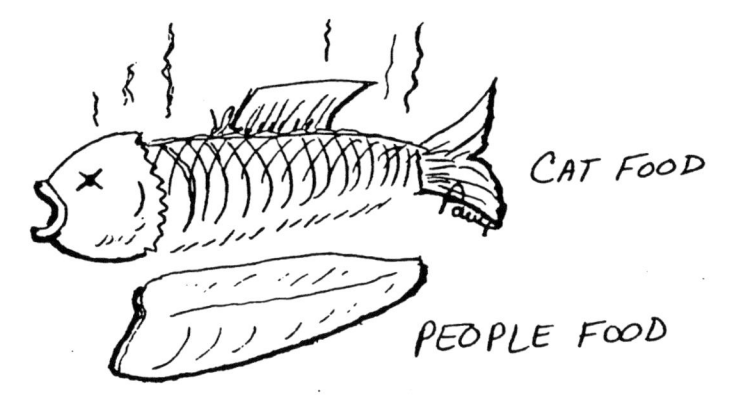

Fish

Just for the sake of it, let's assume that you have been bitten by the fishing bug and have caught this "brain food," not just picked it up, already filleted, at a store. Some fish, such as trout, are traditionally served with their heads still on. If you opt for this, consider covering the eye with a slice of pimento-stuffed olive. There's just something about eating something that's staring back at you, even if it is cooked, that just doesn't help my appetite. Camping and specialty stores sell "fish knives," but a good, sharp regular kitchen knife with a little serration will do the job just as well.

The two best times to get the bones out of a fish are when you are cleaning it fresh, or after it has been cooked and chilled in the ice box, which firms up the flesh enough to get at the bones.

The worst time to debone the fish is when most of us actually do it, while we're eating it hot. The bones have softened from the heat, and the flesh wants to stick to them. Axiom: You will never get all the bones out of these creatures. Just accept it as one of nature's challenges.)

Minnesota Fish Fry

*MC

Traditionally this is cooked in a heavy iron skillet over a campfire, but a kitchen skillet over a Medium-high heat will also do the trick. This recipe is good for any fresh water fish—trout, crappy, bass, pike, etc.—and it is the way to cook catfish. Portions will vary according to the size of the fish.

Corn oil, just enough to cover the skillet bottom
1 T. butter or margarine
Fish fillets
⅓ c. all-purpose flour
½ c. corn meal
1 t. salt
Freshly ground pepper to taste

Heat the oil and butter until the butter foams and just starts to turn brown. Combine the flour, corn meal, salt, and pepper on a plate and dredge the fish fillets, coating both sides. Place the fillets in the skillet, skin side up. Don't crowd them. When the first side is brown, turn the fillets over carefully with a spatula and brown on the other side. Serve at once with lemon wedges and TARTAR SAUCE. Traditional side dishes include hash brown potatoes, hush puppies, cole slaw, sliced tomatoes, and corn on the cob.

Salmon Patties

*MC, F-F

Fresh salmon is great grilled, smoked, or just baked with a little melted margarine and dill or parsley, but for a salmon fix on the cheap, grab a can of salmon at the market. This is another one of those "make the whole darn recipe" recipes. Just slip the leftovers, cooked and cooled,, into a Ziplock bag and zap as needed. Or make enough for your dinner, then form the remainder into small patties, fry, and freeze to use later for an "Impress the Guest" with MEAN MUSTARD SAUCE.

1 can salmon, drained and the bones removed
½ c. mashed potatoes (leftover okay)
1 egg yolk (save the white to add to your next scrambled egg dish)
1 T. parsley flakes
½ t. dried dill weed
¼ c. onion, finely diced
Dash of Tabasco
Ritz crackers crumbs

Smash the salmon in a bowl with a fork. Add all of the other ingredients and stir well until everything is combined. Form into patties and let them rest on a sheet of wax paper for ½ hour or longer. Make cracker crumbs in a blender or crush them in a bag with a rolling pin. PAM a skillet and cover the bottom with vegetable oil. Heat the oil over Medium heat. Pat the crumbs into each side of the salmon patties and slip them carefully into the hot oil. Brown well on both sides and serve with lemon wedges and a little extra parsley. (For a New England touch make frozen creamed peas and use them as a sauce over the patties.)

Everyone's Tuna Casserole
*E

Can there be any child in the USA who has not been served this old stand by? You can fancy it up by adding cooked noodles, water chestnuts, green peas, covering it with garlic crumbs (bread crumbs moistened with garlic butter), or topping it with a little shredded cheese, but it's still tasty, cheap, and easy.

- 1 can tuna fish
- 1 can Campbell's cream of mushroom soup
- ¼ c. onion, diced, optional
- ¼ c. green pepper, diced, optional
- 1 T. margarine, optional
- 1 ½ c. potato chips, crushed

If you opt to use the onion and green pepper, sauté them in the margarine till limp and set aside. Drain the tuna and put it in a bowl. Break it up into little pieces with fork and stir in the soup, straight from the can. Add the onions and green pepper and combine all of the ingredients well. Stir in 1 c. of the potato chips. PAM an aluminum baking pan or casserole and pour in the tuna mixture. Spread the remaining potato chips evenly over the top and bake the casserole in a 350° oven for 30 minutes or until hot and bubbly. Do not add salt! Between the soup and the potato chips there's plenty!

Shrimp

No bones to worry about with the tasty crustaceans—lobster, crab, crayfish, and shrimp. They wear their skeletons outside where you crack it, whack it, or peel it to get the meat. All of these are super just boiled in their shells and served hot with melted butter (or margarine) and lemon or chilled with a lemon/dill mayonnaise. When the beasty turns from its water color, (usually browns ad greens) to its cooked colors (bright red to pink) and you think its done, it's smart to let it boil 5 more minutes to assure thorough cooking.

Fried Shrimp
*E

There are lots of coating mixes in the market, but save yourself the time and hassle. Buy a good brand of precoated frozen shrimp like Mrs. Paul's or Mrs. Friday's, but be freezer smart. Those boxes take up freezer space, so divide the contents into 6-8 shrimp portions and put them in Ziplock bags. You'll save space and be able to see what they are and how many you have.

6–8 frozen shrimp per person

Vegetable oil for frying (this mom likes sunflower oil.)

Heat oil over Medium-high heat. Use tongs to place the shrimp in the hot oil. They should brown fairly slowly so the meat has a chance to thaw and cook. When brown on the first side, turn them over and brown on the second side. Serve with COCKTAIL SAUCE.

Scampi

*MC, FFC

Sounds impressive doesn't it? You'll pay an arm and a leg for it in a restaurant, but you can handle this with no fuss! You can usually buy raw shrimp, fresh or frozen, with their tails on at a large market or a good fish store. If they still have their shells on, just pull off the legs and peel off the shell. To devein the shrimp, take out the black "line" down their backs, which is actually their intestine still filled with dirt and grit, by gently making a small slit down the back and lifting it out. (Some cookbooks will tell you to fish it out with a toothpick, but this is tedious, time consuming, and just plain doesn't work very well!) However, if you get lazy and decide to do without deveining, you will get nasty, gritty shrimp.

6–8 raw shrimp (per person), deveined with their tails still on

2 T. butter or margarine

1 t. garlic purée OR 2 cloves, pressed

1 T. dry white wine, optional (Vermouth is good)

1 t. parsley flakes

PAM a pie plate, individual scallop shells if you want to be fancy, or individual au gratin dishes. Arrange the shrimp in a single layer, close together. Pour the wine over the shrimp if you are using wine. Preheat the oven to 450°. Melt the butter or margarine. Stir in the garlic and the parsley flakes and pour it all over the shrimp. Bake in the hot oven for 5-10 minutes, until the shrimp curl up, turn pink, and are completely opaque. Serve with a nice wedge of lemon.

Shrimp Cabrillo

*MC, FFC

Originally this was served like a shishkabob, with the shrimp and vegetables alternated on a skewer, but the bacon never got completely cooked, and it makes this mother very nervous to eat less than perfectly cooked bacon. To insure that each element is properly cooked, you can wait and combine them at the last moment. It is the combination of all of the flavors with the dipping sauce that will have your guests raving over this dish.

6 raw shrimp (per person), deveined with the tails still on

1 T. butter or margarine

1 t. crushed garlic

6 squares green pepper

6 cubes red onion, cut from the outside layers so that you can get 3 layers per 1″ square

2 T. olive oil

2 strips bacon, microwaved (See Pig In!)

PAM a pie plate or other flat, shallow baking dish. Lay the shrimp on it in a single layer. Preheat the broiler. Melt the butter or margarine, stir in the garlic, and coat the shrimp with the mixture. Heat the olive oil in a small skillet over Medium-high heat. When it becomes hot and fragrant, add the onions and the peppers. Stir until the onions just begin to go limp and the peppers brown and start to blister. Broil the shrimp till curled and done. To serve, place the shrimp on a plate.

Cover each shrimp with a square of cooked onion, a square of cooked green pepper, and ⅓ of a piece of cooked bacon. Serve with a lemon wedge and the warm sauce in a container for dipping.

CABRILLO SAUCE:

1 8 oz. can tomato sauce

⅔ c. ketchup

2 T. Worcestershire sauce

You can warm this by zapping it on medium power or by simmering it in a small PAMMED pan. This recipe will make enough warm sauce for 4 servings of SHRIMP CABRILLO. Freeze any leftover sauce.

Tuna Salad

*F & E

Follow the recipes for HAM SALAD (See Pig In!), substituting tuna for ham. If you like your salad bland or sour, omit the mustard and use a squeeze of lemon with 6–7 stuffed olives, sliced. If you like a sweet tuna salad, just add pickle relish or dice some sweet pickle into the mixture.

Menu Tip: When you serve something with a sweet and spicy sauce like Ribs, FRIED SHRIMP, or SHRIMP CABRILLO, a good partner is a dish with cheese in it like macaroni and cheese or AU GRATIN POTATOES.

Primary
Pasta

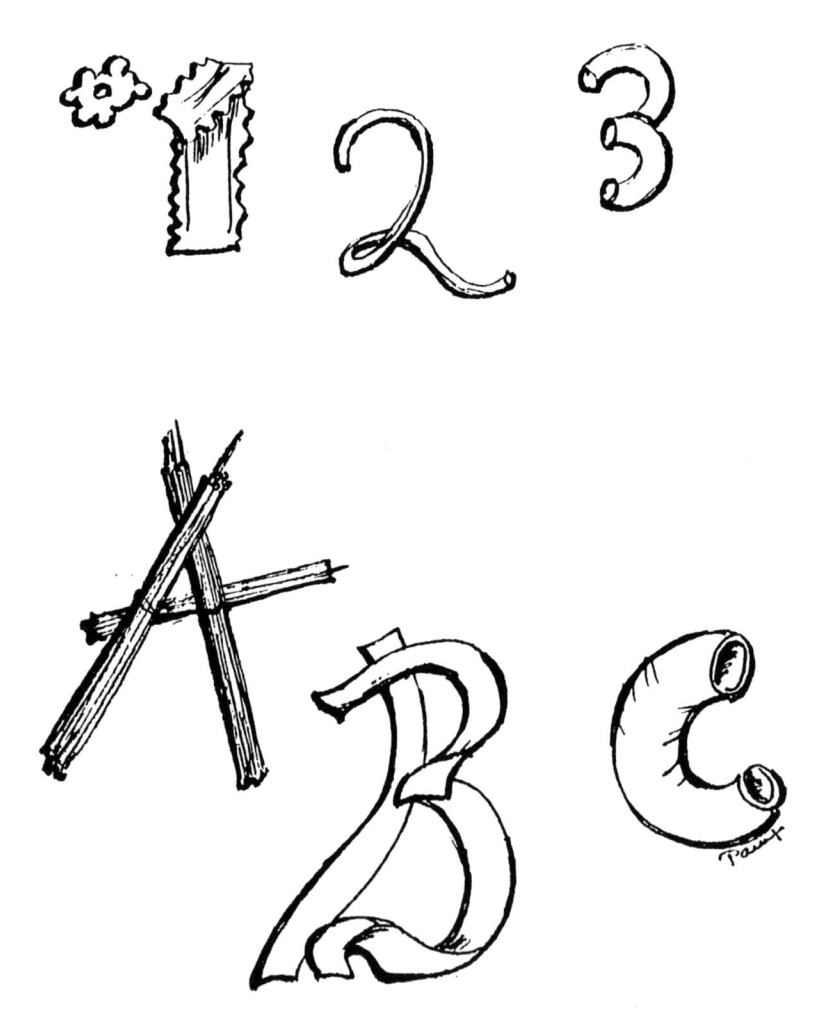

Noodles (and other Pastas)

To precook and revive, follow the package directions (Remember—you CAN read), but you really won't need the gallons of water they usually recommend. 3–4 c. of water with 2 t. of salt and 2 T. of olive oil will be enough unless you are planning to cook more than one whole (16 oz.) package. When the water reaches a rolling boil, add the pasta and stir it around till it goes limp. Start timing the cooking pasta after the water returns to a full boil. Stir the pasta once or twice while it's boiling. (Tip: Stir large pasta, like lasagna noodles, often or they will form a passionate relationship—squishy on the outside, raw on the inside, and permanently glued together!) For some reason the thinner the noodles, the more they seem to prefer to remain unattached until after the saucing.

As soon as the pasta is cooked pour the water and pasta into a colander in the sink. (To tell if pasta is done, you can break a piece in half or bite into a small piece. If it's still crunchy or white in the center, it needs to cook a little longer.) If you are going to use the pasta right away, rinse the pasta under warm water and drain. If you are making it way ahead of time or want to freeze it, toss it with some oil or a couple of tablespoons of margarine. If you want to "preserve" it for an hour or so, rinse the cooking pot, fill it with cold water, and dump the pasta back in. This will stop the cooking and make it cool enough to handle later. It will also keep it from forming any lasting relationships. Drain thoroughly before using the pasta. SAVE LEFTOVER PASTA! It freezes well, zaps back with no negative side effects, and can be the basis for great soups and casseroles!

PASSIONATE PASTA

Unsauced Pasta

No pasta deserves to be eaten totally naked! To eat it without anything is to deny the basic reason for this Chinese dish that Marco Polo took back to Italy. You can buy pasta in just about any shape you can think of from tiny stars to cannelloni tubes, little O's like salad macaroni, to big flat lasagna noodles, all sizes of elbows, shells, et cetera, et cetera, et cetera. But they are all designed to be bathed in something yummy. It can be as simple as olive oil or melted butter with a little garlic or crushed herbs or as complicated as LASAGNA.

Fresh pasta is now available in the deli sections of many supermarkets. It is quicker to cook, usually no more than a minute, but there are still those who swear by the dried varieties that call for a good galloping boil for 10 minutes or more Note: The smaller the pasta, i.e. spaghetini vs. spaghetti, the more sauce it seems to hold...at least it seems that way.

Simple Pasta

*E

For pasta as a side dish, or under something saucy like SWEDISH MEATBALLS, you'll want to keep it simple so that it doesn't compete with the main attraction. Toss the HOT pasta with margarine, olive oil, or butter.

If you want to zip it up a little for a side dish, try a combination of the following (Most will stick to the oil):

Grated Parmesan	Parsley	Poppy Seeds
Crushed Garlic	Chives	Caraway Seeds
Diced Anchovies	Olives	Bacon Bits
Sour Cream	Basil	Pine Nuts

You can also toss your pasta with any variety of good commercial sauces. Buy them in small quantities and experiment to find the ones you like. Your imagination is the limit!

Beyond Spaghetti

You can go beyond the traditional meat sauce! Meatballs! Lasagna! You just need a little help! The following recipes are really fairly simple, good for guests and groups, and freeze well to zap another day.

Linguini Carbonara

*MC, FFC

Cook linguini according to package directions and "preserve it" in cool water till the sauce is finished. Sauce for 2 servings:

4 slices bacon

¼ c. onion, diced

4 mushrooms, sliced and sautéed in olive oil, optional

¼ c. ham, diced (use leftover)

¾ c. whipping cream

1 (3 oz.) package cream cheese

½ c. Jack cheese, grated

¼ c. parmesan, fresh grated

4 oz. brie, without rind, optional

½ t. garlic salt

Freshly ground pepper to taste

PAM a Medium skillet. Fry the bacon until crisp and drain on paper towels. Sauté the diced onion in the bacon fat left in the skillet until transparent but not browned. Add the ham and sauté 2–3 minutes longer. Turn the heat to Low, pour in the cream, and stir, scraping the skillet for brown bits. Break up the cream cheese and add it with the other cheeses to the cream. Cook, stirring until the cheeses have melted and the sauce thickens. Crumble 3 of the bacon strips into the sauce, add the linguini, and toss to coat the pasta completely. Allow the sauce to reheat the pasta. Divide between two plates and crumble half a slice of bacon over each serving.

This is very rich so a green salad with an oil and vinegar dressing or a hot sweet and sour dressing is a good compliment.

ALTERNATIVES: Leave out the bacon and ham. sautéing the onion in 1 T. of olive oil and add ¼ c. of bay shrimp or crab (per person) and 1 T. chives, allowing the meat to heat in the sauce before adding the pasta. Viva **PASTA DEL MAR!**

or

Leave out the bacon and the diced ham and add thin strips of prosciutto ham and small fresh baby peas and you have **PASTA PRIMAVERA**. Be creative!

Stuffed Pasta

*TLC, F-F, FFC

Cook cannelloni, manicotti, or large shell pasta according to package directions and "preserve" them in cool water while you make the filling and preheat the oven to 350°. Once again, make the whole thing and freeze the leftovers. They zap back like a dream!

FILLING:

- 1 small (6–8 oz.) tub ricotta cheese
- 1 egg
- 1 (3 oz.) block cream cheese, softened
- 2 c. mozzarella, shredded
- ¼ c. fresh parmesan, grated
- ½ t. garlic salt
- 2 T. parsley flakes
- Freshly ground pepper to taste

Beat the egg together with the ricotta. This is harder than it sounds because it will take a bit of work! When these are well combined, add all of the remaining ingredients except 1 c. of the mozzarella. (As with lasagna, add cooked spinach to this filling and whatever you make can be christened FLORENTINE.) Remove the pastas from their cool water bath one at a time and drain them well, especially the shells! Using a regular teaspoon, carefully pack the pastas with the filling.

SAUCE: Buy a good commercial tomato sauce, with or without meat, 28 oz. size recommended.

PAM an aluminum roasting pan. Spread 1 c. of the sauce evenly over the bottom. Add the stuffed pasta in a single layer. Pour the remaining sauce evenly over the pasta and sprinkle with the remaining cup of mozzarella. Bake in the middle of a 350° oven for 45 minutes. After you take this dish out of the oven, let it rest for 10 minutes while you toss a salad! Makes 10–12 servings.

Noodles Romanoff

*E

Buy a good commercial brand like Rice-a-Roni or Betty Crocker. Do not necessarily follow the package directions. They change every year or two....Trust ME! Boil the noodles according to the package directions. Return the drained noodles to the pan with the butter called for on the box and return it to the stove over Low heat. Mix the cheese powder with the milk, using a whisk, and stir the liquid into the noodles. Continue stirring till thickened and serve immediately. Freeze leftovers in margarine tubs for individual servings to zap later.

Independent Studies
in
Starches

Starches

We tend to think starch-white. This doesn't really work. Yellow starches—corn and garbanzo beans. Green starches—peas and lima beans. Red starch—kidney beans. You can probably think of more, but the choices in this chapter will stick with a few of the old "tried and trues."

Really Perfect Minute Rice

*E

It looks simple enough to follow on the box directions, and it is! But this is the way to make it a golden, buttery delight. The box directions say this recipe will serve 4, but I KNOW it's just about enough for one really rice-crazed 18–20-year-old male. Adjust the measurements to fit your needs and appetites.

- 1 c. Minute Rice
- 1 c. water
- 1 t. salt
- 1 T. Margarine

Add the salt and the margarine to the water in a PAMMED sauce pan with a lid that fits. Bring the water to a boil over high heat. Add the rice, and when the water returns to a boil, cover the pan and remove it from the heat. Let the rice rest, off of the heat, for 10 minutes. Uncover the rice and stir it with a fork. Spoon 4-6 t. of margarine on top of the rice, sprinkle with additional salt, replace the lid—slightly ajar—and return to the stove over Low heat. Check after 2–3 minutes, and if the margarine has melted, stir well with a wooden spoon to distribute the margarine all through the rice. Serve immediately.

Baked Potato

The all-time side dish—plain or dressed up with the extras: sour cream, chives, crumbled bacon, cheese, nacho sauce...You name it, and someone has probably put it on a baked potato!

Basic Baked

*E

- 1 baking potato per person
- **Margarine or butter**
- **Salt and pepper to taste**

Scrub the potato under warm water with a stiff brush to remove any dirt still hiding in the valleys. Dry thoroughly. Using a dinner or salad fork, pierce the skin all over.

(The steam has to be able to escape while the spud cooks, or it will build up under the skin and explode hot potato all over your oven.)

Smear the outside with margarine and bake on an aluminum baking sheet for 1 hour at 425°.

Turn the potato over 30 minutes through the cooking time. Take the potato out of the oven with hot pads and gently squeeze it to start breaking up the insides and soften it before you slit it open and add more margarine or butter and salt and pepper to taste. This is a purist's potato, but most people will now want to pile on the goodies listed above. Save the skin, if you can resist the temptation, for POTATO SKINS.

Dennis Day Potatoes

*MC, FFC

The ultimate stuffed or twice baked potato. When you want to sound like a French gourmet, you can call them "Pommes St. Denis," but no matter what name you choose, these potatoes are an easy way to win raves! They are an absolutely perfect companion for a good steak and thrifty too—one potato serves two. While these do not freeze well or zap well because of the varying densities of the ingredients, they will live in the icebox for 3–4 days and reheat in the oven.

- 1 BASIC BAKED POTATO for 2 people
- 1 T. butter or margarine
- Salt and pepper to taste
- 2 T. sour cream
- 1 T. chives (freeze dried or fresh)
- 1 T. red onion, finely diced
- ⅓ c. sharp cheddar cheese, cut in small cubes (Grated cheese will not work. It doesn't create the same flavor, and it melts too fast.)
- 2 strips of bacon, microzapped

No need to "soften" the baked potato as you take it out of the oven. Have the butter or margarine ready in a Medium-sized mixing bowl. Cut the potato in half the long way and scoop the pulp into the bowl. Mash the potato and the butter together with a fork, adding salt and pepper to taste. Stir in the sour cream, chives, and onions, combining well . Stir in the cheese, pile into the remaining skins, stud with the bacon, breaking it into bits. Bake at 350° till the cheese begins to melt, approximately 15 minutes.

Potatoes Au Gratin

*MC, FFC

"Au Gratin" simply means topped with cheese, but we all know these as the cheesy, creamy, perfect combination of potatoes, sliced or shredded, baked crispy on top. Perfect with FRIED SHRIMP, BBQ, or grilled meat. (Cheese is always a good contrast to any sweet or tomato based sauce.) This recipe serves 2–3 but can easily be expanded. (The "instant", boxed variety are okay, but fresh is better.)

- 1 c. shredded potatoes (patties thawed or the sacked kind from the deli section)
- 2 thin slices of onion, cut in halves
- 1 c. cheddar cheese, coarsely shredded
- ½ c. whipping cream

Salt and freshly ground pepper to taste

PAM a 3 c. baking dish. Spread ⅓ c. of the potatoes in the dish. Arrange ½ of the onion slices over the potatoes. Sprinkle with salt and pepper and cover with ⅓ c. of the cheese. Repeat with ⅓ c. more potatoes, the remaining onion, salt, pepper, and ⅓ c. of the cheese. Add the last ⅓ c. potatoes. Pour the cream evenly over the potatoes and cover with the last ⅓ c. of cheese. Bake uncovered in a 325° oven for 1 hour.

Mashed Potatoes

*F&E, FFC

BUY THE INSTANT! Just don't let any purists in the kitchen to see what you're doing!! They will never know the difference unless you tell them. Prepare the potatoes following the directions on the box, but use CREAM instead of milk and keep the cream out of the icebox. As the potatoes get dry and begin to pull away from the pan, add more cream till they reach the consistency you like. Push a goodly blob of margarine in the center of each serving and sprinkle with paprika. Voilà!

Boiled New Potatoes

*E

Buy the tiniest, firmest red potatoes you can find. Scrub them thoroughly under running water to remove any bits of dirt. Cut in half any potatoes that seem too large.

4–6 baby new potatoes per serving

water

2 T. margarine

1 T. parsley flakes

1 t. dried or fresh chives

Place the potatoes in a sauce pan and cover with water. Bring to a boil and cook the potatoes 20 minutes or until tender when pierced with a fork. Turn the heat to Low. Drain the potatoes and return them to the pan with the margarine, parsley, and chives. Place over the Low heat and put a lid on loosely, as some steam will escape from the boiled potatoes. Heat 10 minutes, clamp the lid on tightly, and shake the pot vigorously to "toss" the potatoes. Heat 10 minutes more and serve with the browned herb butter from the pot.

French Fries And Potato Salad

*E

You are trying to figure out what these two have in common, right? Simple, they are both labor intense, a pain to make right, and not worth the effort when you can buy them at a very reasonable price. You will probably never want to invest in enough oil, a professional quality fryer, and the resulting mess that any Mickey D's or Gag-in-the-Bag uses daily. Frozen fries might be a little less than perfect, but bake them according to the directions on the bag, and you will have an edible potato with quantums less oil and cholesterol! As for POTATO SALAD, just find a brand you like, buy it at the local market or deli, or doctor your own. To "doctor" potato salad:

Buy as much potato salad as you think you'll use. Dump it into a mesh strainer or colander and rinse it well under HOT water to get rid of the dressing. Shake off all of the liquid and put the hot potatoes in a bowl. Add a few squirts of mustard and stir to barely coat all of the pieces. Set aside to cool. When cooled, add Miracle Whip, sweet pickle relish, and diced celery to taste. Chill at least 2 hours to blend the flavors and sprinkle each serving with a little paprika for color.

Hashed Browns

Basically these are fried (sautéed) potatoes that can come in several forms: shredded, either loose or in cakes; country-style, chunks or cubes; home-style, chunks or slices. They or may not have onions. If you add onions, green peppers, and sometimes a little pimiento to cubed hashed browns you have created POTATOES O'BRIEN. If you add onions to sliced, fried potatoes, you'll get the French classic POMMES LYONAISSE. Once again, especially for the shredded variety, buy them frozen or in the newer "fresh" sacked type from the deli section. For the sliced, chunk, or cubed varieties, you can buy them frozen or do them yourself. Buy red (new) potatoes or White Rose, the yellow waxy kind. Baking potatoes will just turn to mush! Tips for Cooking:

1. Use a combination of vegetable oil and butter or margarine. The oil will keep the buttery spread from burning, but the butter/margarine gives it flavor.
2. Cook them slowly over Medium to Medium-high heat. Don't fuss with them. You get the nice crisp crust by letting them brown evenly before turning.
3. If you want to add onions and/or peppers, let the potatoes get a head start. When you think the potatoes are about half done on the first side, sprinkle the veggies evenly over the top. Most of them should end up on the bottom of the pan when you turn the potatoes over.
4. If you decide on POTATOES O'BRIEN, or any cubed potatoes, you can stir them more often, but remember the vegetables will take about ½ the cooking time and don't add the diced pimiento until right before serving. If you try to cook the already processed pimientos with the potatoes, you will end up with some pink, mushy potatoes instead of little red, color spots.

You don't need to peel potatoes, save yourself the time and keep the vitamins.

Potato Skins
*E

Serve whole as a side dish or cut into two bite-size pieces for "Impress the Guests."

- ½ **baked potato skin per person**
- ¼ **c. sharp cheddar cheese, shredded**
- 1 **T. sliced green onion, approximately 1 onion**
- 1 **slice nuked bacon, crumbled**
- **Sour cream**
- **Salsa (see "Impress the Guests")**

Cover the skin evenly with the cheese. Sprinkle with the onions and the bacon. Bake at 375° until the cheese has melted completely. Top each with a dollop of sour cream and pass the salsa. As an appetizer, serve the sour cream and the salsa in separate bowls and let the guests help themselves.

Corn On The Cob
*E

Okay, you can buy this frozen, but it is **never** good as real, fresh corn that is usually in season from late spring to early fall. Corn can be yellow or white and some people swear by one or the other, but they're both great if FRESH! A good, ripe ear of corn will have good kernels all the way to the top of the cob, and if you pop a kernel with your finger nail, it should break easily with a creamy white liquid "milk." Just shuck the corn, trim off the stalk end at the base of the cob, and boil it for 15 minutes. Don't add anything to the water. If you add salt, it will toughen the kernels and turn them a darker yellow. Even if you don't like corn on the cob because of the membranes that can get stuck in your teeth, make it fresh and cut it off the cob with a sharp, serrated knife. Use leftovers in one of the following recipes.

Mexi-Corn
*MC, FFC, F-F

Sure you can buy this canned or frozen, but once again this is much better fresh!

- 1 **c. fresh-cut corn off the cob (cooked or raw)**
- ¼ **c. diced red onion**
- 2 **T. diced green pepper**
- 1 **T. diced pimiento or red tomato skin**
- 1 **T. butter or margarine**
- 1 **t. corn oil**
- ½ **t. chili powder**

Heat oil and sauté onions and peppers over Medium heat till they just start to turn limp. Add the corn and the chili powder and continue to cook, stirring occasionally for another 10–12 minutes. Stir in pimiento or tomato skin and cook 1 minute longer. Serves 2 and freezes well.

Corn Fritters

*MC, FFC

Great with ham or fried chicken as a side dish or with bacon as an alternative to the traditional breakfast pancakes.

½ c. freshly scraped raw corn or 1 small can yellow corn mashed with a potato masher

1 egg

3 T. flour

Dash of nutmeg

2 T. butter

Heat butter over Medium heat till fragrant. Beat the egg into the corn till it is completely combined. Add the remaining ingredients and mix well. Drop the batter into the hot butter with a tablespoon. Brown the bottom of each fritter, turn and brown on the other side, and serve with honey or maple syrup. Makes 8–9 fritters.

Baked Beans

*E, FFC

This recipe serves 2, But you can expand it to serve a mob, cheaply. Put the leftovers in the icebox because these are just as good cold!

1 (8 oz.) can pork and beans

1 T. onion, diced

1 T. ketchup

1 t. brown sugar

1 t. molasses

2 t. Real Bacon Bits

1 squirt prepared mustard

PAM a baking dish—aluminum is good because you will probably want to pitch it. Combine all of the ingredients and pour into the dish. Mix 1 T. more of ketchup with a little water to make a thin tomato sauce and pour over the top. Bake at 325° for 1 hour.

Green Bean Casserole

*E, FFC

Yet another staple of the infamous pot luck, but it's still a handy recipe for a mob-feed of any kind. Leftovers can be frozen and zapped back with decent results.

2 (10 oz.) frozen French-cut green beans

1 can Campbell's cream of mushroom soup

⅓ soup can of milk

1 t. curry powder

1 small can Durkee's fried onions

1 small can (7–8 oz.) sliced water chestnuts (or use the leftovers from a Chinese dinner, sliced or chopped)

Cook the green beans according to the directions on the box. PAM a baking dish. In a mixing bowl combine the soup, milk, and curry powder to make the sauce. Drain the green beans and stir into the sauce. Add half the can of fried onions, breaking them with your hand, and the water chestnuts. Stir to combine well. Pour the beans into the baking dish and cover the top evenly with the remaining fried onions, crumbled. Bake at 325° for 25–30 minutes and serve hot.

Impress the Guests with a Dead Hot Dog and Other Lovable Leftovers

Everyone has at least one DEAD HOT DOG in their icebox. You know the one I'm talking about—the lone little doggy that slipped to the back of the meat drawer. It's just unappealing in its singularity. There's nothing really wrong with it yet. It hasn't turned green and slimy or dried out beyond recognition, yet it sits there in accusatory silence. Turn that dog into a minor triumph, especially if you can combine it with those two of slices of bologna, that drying hunk of salami, that one slice of cheese, and the stray olive or pickle taking up an entire jar. Use these all together and you can put together a small "Impress the Guests" hot and cold set of nibblers to precede your dinner. Everyone has that hot dog in their past, or their future, but YOU can turn it into a lovable treat!

One Dead Hot Dog

*F&E, FFC

1 dead hot dog, thinly sliced

½ c. of BBQ sauce, one from this book OR a commercial sauce you like OR you can try this one from more "leftovers":

¼ c. red jelly (strawberry, currant, etc.)

¼ c. prepared mustard

Heat the jelly and the mustard together in a small sauce pan over Low heat, stirring until the jelly melts and the sauce is well combined. Stir in the hot dog slices, turn into a microwave-safe container (like a Pyrex custard cup) and zap on Medium-low for 30–60 seconds. Serve warm with frilly toothpicks. (Use the same method for heating in any of the sauces.) You won't need to keep this small a quantity on a warmer as they will disappear too fast! Of course you can use the same recipe for a larger batch, for mini hot dogs, or for smoky links. Serve with something "cheesy" like stuffed celery, a cheddar spread, or tortilla chips with melted cheese (found later in this chapter).

Other HOT tidbits for the preshow might include LAMB RIBLETS, SWEET AND SOUR RIBS, MINI SALMON PATTIES, or any of the MEATBALL recipes. How about some of that leftover HAM SLICE?

Hot Ham Kabobs

*MC, FFC,

Allow 2 kabobs per person. For each kabob, assemble:

3 cubes of ham

2 pineapple chunks

2 squares of green pepper

On a bamboo skewer, small metal skewer (poultry pins work well), or a long toothpick without frills, string 1 green pepper square, 1 ham cube, 1 pineapple chunk, followed by ham, pineapple, ham, and the last green pepper. Broil close to he heat for 2-3 minutes. Turn over and broil the other side. Serve hot with MEAN MUSTARD SAUCE or any good commercial mustard for dipping.

Nuked Chinese Nibblers

*MC, FFC, M

You can also call these "Poor People's Rumaki" because real rumaki calls for chunks of chicken livers which add to the fuss and cooking time and which lots of people don't like, believing that liver isn't human food.

For each serving allow:
- **4 whole water chestnuts**
- **1 strip of bacon**
- **1 toothpick**

Starting at one end of the bacon strip and finishing with the other end, weave the bacon and the water chestnuts onto the toothpick. Cover a paper plate with at least two paper towels and place the nibblers around the plate in a circle with the bacon flat, not on edge. Zap on High for 30 seconds times the number of bacon strips. Remove from the oven, turn each nibbler over, and zap again for 30 seconds per slice. Now you have to nuke at your own discretion. They will not probably be done at this point, but each batch of bacon cooks at its own speed so keep rotating the plate and zapping them with 30-second shots till they suit your taste. Serve with sweet and sour sauce and some of the Chinese hot mustard you saved from your last take-out. Raw veggie chunks with ranch dressing compliment these nicely.

Walking Potatoes

*MC, FFC

Don't let the caviar in this recipe throw you! Decent—not necessarily good or great—domestic caviars (fish eggs from lumpfish are now readily available in most large markets. Whitefish caviar looks the same, but it is very gooey and harder to work with. Look in the canned fish section at the market for red, black, or golden domestic caviars. The salmon roe, large-egged red, and the black lumpfish usually found chilled in the deli section are usually twice the cost!) You can also use these caviars as an elegant topping for DEVILED EGGS or in a cream cheese dip.

- **2 small red new potatoes per person, scrubbed, dried, pierced, and baked like a regular BAKED POTATO, but for only 10–12 minutes on each side.**
- **Sour cream**
- **Caviar**
- **Chives (dried or fresh)**

Cut each baked new potato in half. Turn them cut-side up and spoon a small dollop of sour cream on each side. With the tip of a knife push a goodly glob of caviar into the center of the sour cream, sprinkle with chives, and serve hot.

Mexican Pizza

*E, FFC

Also known as a "cheese crisp," this comes in two basic styles. "Pizza" is usually based on a large flour tortilla and cut into wedges while the "crisp" is usually on a tostada, a crisply fried corn tortilla. Fold either one over with the cheese of your choice inside, and you have a QUESIDILLA. Add sour cream, SALSA, or GUACAMOLE, and you have a super starter. Add refried beans and/or taco meat, and it's a meal!

PIZZA

You can use a small flour tortilla for one or a larger tortilla that you cut into wedges for 3 or more.

> 1 flour tortilla
> Corn oil
> Colby, Jack, or cheddar cheese, shredded
> Ortega green chilies (Whole, rinsed, and cut into strips for a mild chili flavor or diced for a hotter result)
> 1 green onion, thinly sliced

Brush or smear one side of the tortilla with the corn oil and place it, oiled side down, on a PAMMED cookie sheet large enough to hold it. Sprinkle the cheese(s) of your choice evenly over the tortilla. Lay the chili strips over the cheese or sprinkle with diced chilies to taste. Sprinkle with the onion and bake in a 450° oven just until the cheese melts and bubbles on the edges. The bottom should be browned and crisp. Slice into wedges and serve with sour cream, SALSA, and GUACAMOLE.

CHEESE CRISPS

Tostados (flat, fried, corn tortillas) are available at the market, but you might as well make your own because it is so easy and they do taste better. Just buy fresh corn tortillas and brown each side over Medium-high heat in enough corn oil to cover the bottom of the skillet. Cut the tortillas into wedges before you fry them and you have your own tortilla chips. Salt them. Simple!

> 1 corn tortilla, whole or cut in half and fried crisp
> Shredded cheddar cheese
> ½ Ortega chili, cut into long strips
> 1 green onion, sliced

Sprinkle the tortilla evenly with the cheese. Add the onion and then layer on the chili strips. Bake in a 350° oven until the cheese melts and is bubbly. Serve with SALSA, sour cream, and GUACAMOLE as an appetizer or use these as a great side dish with chili.

Chili Con Queso

*F&E, FFC

An easy hot dip that you can microzap or heat on the stove. These are ingredients that you can keep on hand and whip together in a couple of minutes.

1 (8 oz.) block Velveeta cheese food

¼ c. commercial salsa (Don't use fresh salsa for this because it is a little too sour and juicier than the commercial products.)

Melt the cheese food. Stir in the salsa. Heat just long enough to incorporate and heat the salsa. Keep warm and serve with tortilla chips for dipping.

Hot Artichoke Dip

*MC, FFC

People will beg you for this recipe. It has one expensive ingredient. The artichoke bottoms should cost about $3.00, but the end result is worth it! Use canned artichoke bottoms packed in water. DO NOT use the marinated, salad artichoke hearts.

1 (7–8 oz.) can artichoke bottoms
1 (4 oz.) can Ortega diced green chilies
2 c. Best Foods mayonnaise
2 c. Kraft dry parmesan cheese
1 t. garlic salt
1 t. Worcestershire sauce

PAM an aluminum or Pyrex baking dish. Drain the artichoke bottoms and dice them. Do not drain the chilies. Combine all of the ingredients in a large bowl and pour into the baking dish. Bake at 350° oven for 30 minutes. Keep warm and serve hot with spoons to transfer the dip to Triskets.

COLD APPETIZERS: Once again, take a hard look through your icebox, and you'll probably find enough for a pre-dinner snack for 2–4 people: a couple of celery stalks, cheeses, luncheon meats, etc.

Stack-Ups & More

*MC, F&E, FFC

Bologna, American cheese, bologna, and a chunk of sweet pickle. Stack the meat and cheese. Cut into 8 little pie shapes. Top each one with pickle piece. Stab a frilly toothpick through, and you have 8 nibblers.

A cube of salami, a cube of Jack or cheddar cheese, and a stuffed olive or a pickled onion run through with a frilly pick.

Apple wedges with any kind of cheese.

Two stalks of celery filled with peanut butter or cheese spread, cut into 8 pieces.

Any creamy salad dressing, (ranch, Italian, Caesar, etc.) or some mayonnaise with a little curry powder or dill weed, and you have an instant dip for any raw veggies you may have in the crisper. Cut them into bite-size pieces, and you now have CRUDITES & DIP.

A little time to prepare, but not enough to get to the store? Make DEVILED EGGS. (See Fowlproof Fowl)

Those Sour Cream Dips

*****F&E, FFC,**

ONION: 1 (16 oz.) container of sour cream mixed well with 1 envelope Lipton onion soup mix.

VEGGIE: 1 (16 oz.) container of sour cream mixed well with 1 envelope of any dry vegetable soup (without noodles!)

BLUE CHEESE: 1 (16 oz) container of sour cream mixed well with 4 oz. of crumbled blue cheese and a dash of Worcestershire sauce.

B/H: 1 (8 oz.) container of sour cream mixed well with 1 T. prepared horseradish and 3 T. Real bacon bits or 6 strips of crisply zapped bacon, crumbled

CHEDDAR CHILI: 1 (8 oz.) container of sour cream mixed well with 1 c. shredded sharp cheddar cheese and 2 t. chili powder

All dips taste better if they can sit in the icebox for an hour or two before serving to allow the flavors to blend.

Cream Cheese

Soft varieties are now available in almost any flavor anyone could want, but the old method of softening a regular block of cream cheese still seems to taste better and have a better dipping consistency. You can soften cream cheese very easily in the microwave. Remove it from its foil wrapper and put it into a microwave-safe bowl. Zap it on Low for 30 seconds at a shot till it's soft enough to blend well—room temperature. Not hot!

Cream Cheese And Olive Dip

*****F&E, FFC**

1 (8 oz.) block of Philadelphia cream cheese

1 t. onion, finely diced

1 t. chives, sliced

½ c. stuffed olives, sliced

Thin the softened cream cheese with enough olive juice to reach a dipping consistency. Stir in the onions and chives well and then gently stir in the olive slices. Chill it in the icebox for at least ½ hour, if possible.

"Smoked" Salmon Paté

*MC, F-F, FFC

Very rich, this spread tastes like you've spent half your monthly food bill on lox, the royalty of smoked salmon.

- 1 (7½ oz.) can red salmon
- 2 (3 oz.) packages of Philadelphia cream cheese
- 1 T. butter (not margarine!)
- 1 t. dill weed
- 1 T. parsley flakes
- 1 T. red onion, finely diced
- 2 T. celery, finely diced
- ½ t. liquid smoke
- 1 t. lemon juice

In a mixing bowl allow the cream cheese and the butter to soften to room temperature. Combine the butter and the cream cheese thoroughly. (Butter is part of the key to this recipe. It makes the paté firm when chilled, and it makes it possible to freeze any leftovers. Cream cheese cannot be frozen without deteriorating unless butter is added to it.) Drain the salmon and remove all the bones possible. Smash it well into the cream cheese. If the salmon is pale in color and you want to perk it up, add 1 drop of red food coloring and 2 drops of yellow food coloring and stir till the color is evenly distributed. Repeat if necessary. Now add all of the remaining ingredients and combine well. Mound the spread onto a larger plate and smooth into a hemisphere. Sprinkle with chopped parsley or parsley flakes or stud the surface with SPICED PECANS. Refrigerate for at least an hour and serve with Ritz crackers.

Spiced Pecans

*TLC, FFC

- ½ c. pecan halves
- 2 T. margarine or butter
- 1 t. curry powder
- ½ t. garlic powder
- Garlic salt to taste

Melt the margarine over Medium heat then add the garlic powder and the curry powder. Cook together, stirring for 1 minute. Add the pecan halves and stir to coat well. Pour the pecans onto a baking sheet in a single layer and bake at 225° for 30 minutes, stirring occasionally, and sprinkling with garlic salt. Let the nuts cool completely and store in an airtight container till needed. These will keep about 2 weeks without refrigeration, if you can keep them around that long!

Seasoned Cream Cheese

*F&E, FFC

For a small batch of nibblers, this one can be doubled, tripled, and on, and on, and on...

1 (3 oz.) package Philadelphia cream cheese
½ t. Worcestershire sauce
¼ t. celery salt

Soften the cream cheese and stir in the remaining ingredients well. Use to stuff celery, form into little balls, chill to use later as a nice touch on a tossed green salad, or use for CHIPPED BEEF ROLL-UPS or SALAMI CORNUCOPIAS.

Chipped Beef Roll-Ups

*MC, FFC

1 (4½ oz) jar dried chipped beef
1 recipe SEASONED CREAM CHEESE

Separate the chipped beef into circles and overlap the slices in two rows, 3 wide and 6 long. Spread half of the cream cheese gently over the slices to cover. Roll the slices from the short end to form a tube. Wrap tightly in Saran Wrap and refrigerate. Repeat. (If you want to, make a whole batch of these and freeze them, but remember to add butter to the cream cheese!) Let the rolls chill for at least 1 hour and then cut into slices with a sharp knife. Serve immediately or chill till serving time.

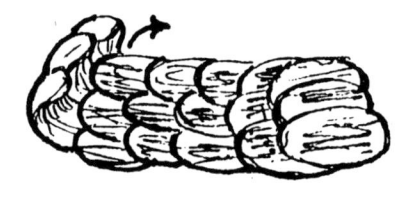

Salami Cornucopias

*MC, FFC

You will find these on the fanciest trays of canapés, but the fancy piped filling will taste just as good smeared in with a butter knife and decorated with an olive slice.

4 slices of Oscar Mayer's hard salami
1 recipe SEASONED CREAM CHEESE

Spread each slice with a little of the cream cheese. Cut each slice in half and roll into a cone with the cream cheese on the inside. Secure at the base with frilly toothpick. Use the rest of the cream cheese to fill the cornucopia and chill.

Simply Smashing Seafood Spread

*F&E, FFC

1 (8 oz.) block Philadelphia cream cheese
⅔–1 c. canned crab meat or fresh (cooked) bay shrimp are the most affordable
¼ c. celery, finely diced
1 c. COCKTAIL SAUCE

Unwrap the cream cheese onto a large plate with a rim (like pie pan), cover with Saran Wrap, and let it come to almost room temperature. Drain and rinse the seafood(s) and combine well with the cocktail sauce and diced celery. Pour the seafood cocktail evenly over the cream cheese and serve immediately with Ritz crackers. Cut down through the sauce and cheese to get both to spread on the cracker. Very rich and VERY IMPRESSIVE! But BUDGET WISE!

Cheddachut Spread

*F&E, FFC

1 (8 oz.) container cold pack cheddar cheese food—like Wisepride, K-K, or Kraft
2 T. chutney

Spoon the cheese into a microwave-safe bowl. Zap on Low for 30 seconds to just barely soften it. Spoon the chutney onto a small plate and cut any large pieces into tiny pieces. Stir the chutney into the cheese and repack in a crock or the original container. Chill for at least one hour before serving with assorted crackers. Wheat Thins are really good with this spread.

SAUCES AND SUCH: One of the easiest ways to "dress up" even the simplest dish is to serve it either in or with a good sauce. Some of you may quibble that guacamole is really a dip, but it becomes a sauce on taquitos and other Mexican dishes. Oriental sauces are a little complicated to make so the suggestion here is that you buy your hoisin, plum sauce, or sweet and sour sauce in the Oriental section of the market. Just about every place carries La Choy if not a few more exotic numbers.

Cocktail Sauce

*F&E, FFC

Simple, simple, simple but GOOOOOOOD!

¾ c. Heinz chili sauce
3 T. lemon juice
1 T. prepared horseradish

or if you want a smaller batch for 2 people:

¼ c. Heinz chili sauce
1 T. lemon juice
1 t. prepared horseradish

Combine all of the ingredients well and use as a sauce for Shrimp Cocktail or as a dipping sauce for FRIED SHRIMP.

Tartar Sauce

*E, FFC

Perfect for virtually every fish as well as abalone and scallops.

½ c. Best Foods mayonnaise
1 T. lemon juice
1 T. onion, diced
1 T. dill pickles, diced or dill relish
2 t. chopped capers, optional
6 sour cocktail onions, diced
1 T. parsley flakes

Thin the mayonnaise with the lemon juice and stir in the rest of the ingredients. Let the sauce chill in the icebox for at least an hour to blend the flavors. Do not try to short cut by substituting sweet pickle relish—BLAAAAH!

Mean Mustard Sauce

*E, FFC

Start with a good commercial mustard like French's or Gulden's but warn your guests that this mustard has a little extra kick.

¼ c. prepared mustard
1 T. Best Foods mayonnaise
1 t. Coleman's dry mustard
½ t, sugar
1 t. water
1 t. dill weed

Combine mustard and mayonnaise in a small bowl. In a separate bowl (or custard cup) combine the dry mustard, sugar, and water and stir till the sugar dissolves. Let this mixture sit for at least 15 minutes. It will thicken slightly. Add the mustard/sugar to the mustard and mayonnaise and stir to combine well. Stir in the dill and chill for at least 30 minutes to blend the flavors. This is good on fish and vegetables. Omit the dill and add 1 t. prepared horseradish, and you have a good mustard for sausages and other meats.

Salsa Fresca

*E, FFC

Great as a dip, on tacos or tostadoes. Whirl in a blender for instant gaspacho (Spanish cold tomato soup), and it keeps for 2–3 weeks in the icebox.

1 onion slice, diced (about ⅓ c.)
Lime juice to cover
Garlic salt to taste

This is the trick. Put the diced onion in a glass jar with a tightly fitting lid. Just barely cover the onion with lime juice and sprinkle generously with garlic salt. Put the lid on the jar and store in the icebox overnight. This mellows the onion and gives this salsa its distinctive taste. Add

- 1 T. corn oil
- 1 tomato, diced
- ½ green pepper, diced
- ⅓ cucumber, peeled, seeded, and diced, optional
- ½c. La Victoria Salsa Suprema, medium hot

If you have any whole Ortega chilies hanging around, dice ½ of a chili and throw that in too. Put everything in the jar. Tighten the lid and shake vigorously to combine everything well. Store in the icebox till ready to use.

Guacamole

*E, FFC

At it's simplest, guacamole is

- 1 ripe avocado, peeled, seeded, and mashed with
- 1–2 T. mayonnaise
- 1 t. lime juice, or to taste
- Garlic salt to taste
- Dash of Tabasco sauce

To stretch it or make it chunkier, you might want to add any or all of the following:

Diced tomato	Chili powder
Diced Ortega chilies	Taco Sauce
Dash of Worcestershire	

To serve, pile the guacamole in a bowl. Make a well in the center with the back of a spoon. Spoon some SALSA FRESCA in the center for added flavor and a color accent. Serve with tortilla chips.

Antipasto

*MC, FFC

A bit of this and a bit of that presented on a pretty platter, and you have the perfect introduction for any Italian meal or light meal by itself with some good GARLIC BREAD.

- 4 large Romaine lettuce leaves
- 1 (6 oz.) jar marinated artichoke hearts, chilled
- 4 oz. mozzarella cheese, cubed
- 4 oz. Italian salami cubed, or if already sliced, cut into wedges
- 1 (3½ oz.) can whole black olives, pitted
- 1 (12–16 oz.) jar Gardiner pickled vegetables, chilled, optional
- 1 (3½ oz.) jar Italian roasted peppers, optional
- 8 Vlasic pepperoncini salad peppers

1 ripe tomato, cut into 8 wedges
Italian dressing

Arrange the lettuce leaves on an attractive large plate or small platter. Place the tomato in the center. Arrange the cheese, meat, and vegetables. Drain any marinades and combine them with the dressing. Spoon liberally over all the ingredients. Cover with plastic wrap and chill for up to 2 hours or serve immediately.

Garlic Bread El Cheapo

*E, FFC

Split a French roll in two and pretend it's the real thing or stretch one loaf into 2.

1 loaf of unsliced French bread
1 (8 oz.) tub of margarine
2 T. crushed garlic
Parmesan cheese, optional

With a serrated knife split the loaf of bread in half the long way. Cut into slices almost all the way through. Thoroughly mix the margarine and the garlic together. Divide the garlic butter evenly between the two half loaves pushing some down between each slice. Place the loaves on a baking sheet and sprinkle with the Parmesan cheese. Broil until the tops are nicely browned and serve hot.

Gourmet Garlic Bread

*E, FFC

1 loaf of *sliced* French bread
1 tub of margarine (8 oz.)
½ stick of butter, softened
2 T. crushed garlic
1 T. parsley flakes
1 sheet of heavy duty aluminum foil, slightly longer than the loaf of bread.

Mix the margarine, butter, garlic, and parsley together well. The parsley flakes will give you a good indicator when the butter is well mixed. Spread the butter on the top ⅔ of each slice, both sides, and reassemble the loaf on the foil. Reserve about 1 T. of the butter to spread on the top. Wrap the foil up and around the loaf but so that the top is still open. Bake in a 350° oven for 20 minutes or until the top just starts to brown. Serve hot.

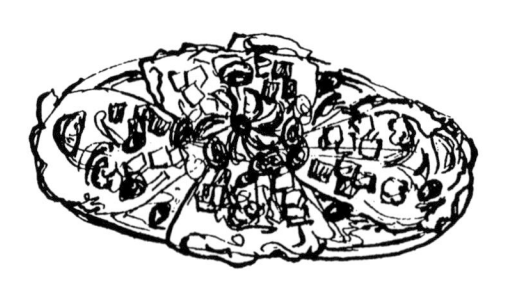

Desserts With (And Without) Leftovers

Desserts have always been a great way to "Impress the Guests" and these are cheap, easy, and the first two use "leftovers." Keep your parents out of the kitchen or make these desserts ahead of time, and they'll wonder where you've found the time to take cooking classes!

Buñuelos

*F&E, FFC

Extra flour tortillas leftover? Use them for this classic Mexican dessert. You can serve these plain or with a scoop of vanilla ice cream in the center.

- **Flour tortillas**
- **Oil for frying (Not corn oil, but a lighter vegetable oil will work)**
- **Cinnamon sugar (Mix granulated sugar with ground cinnamon to taste. The more cinnamon you add, the "hotter" it will be.)**
- **Vanilla ice cream, optional**

Heat the oil in a medium skillet over medium-high heat. Brown the tortillas in the oil one at a time, turning to brown both sides. Drain on paper towels and sprinkle generously with the cinnamon sugar. Keep warm in a low, 200° oven. Serve with or without ice cream.

Rice Pudding

*E

Have some half'n'half or whipping cream ready to pour over this warm pudding from the oven, and you'll feel like you're six years old again.

- **1 c. cooked rice (leftover Minute Rice is okay!)**
- **⅔ c. milk**
- **3 T. sugar**
- **2 t. melted butter**
- **½ t. vanilla**
- **2 eggs**
- **½ t. lemon juice**
- **¼ c. raisins**

PAM a 3 c. baking dish. In a medium bowl beat the eggs with the sugar till it dissolves then stir in the vanilla, milk, and lemon juice. Add the rice and stir well. Add the butter and the raisins and make sure they are distributed throughout the pudding. Pour into the baking dish and sprinkle with cinnamon. Bake in the middle of a 325° oven for 30 minutes or until firm in the center when you give it a little jiggle. I've heard some people call this the warm dessert equivalent of vanilla ice cream.

Apple Brown Betty

*E

This short cut version may seem like cheating, but it's so easy and so good, who cares?!

1 package Stouffer's escalloped apples, thawed

¼ c. raisins

4 slices white or French bread, crumbled

3 T. margarine, melted

1 T. sugar

PAM a baking pan (aluminum suggested). Stir the raisins into the thawed apples and pour into the prepared pan. Pour the margarine over the bread crumbs and mix well till all the crumbs are moistened. (If it still seems dry, add more melted margarine.) Stir in the sugar and sprinkle the buttered crumbs evenly over apples. You may have to use your fingers to get an even coating. Bake at 350° for 30 minutes or until the "crust" is brown. Serve warm with a splash of whipping cream, goodly squirt of whipped cream, or a scoop of vanilla ice cream.

Whipped Cream Cake

*E, TLC

This makes a nice birthday cake for 4–6 people, and you can tailor it to the taste of the guest of honor.

1 small Sara Lee all butter pound cake, thawed

1 pt. ice cream or sherbet

1 (7 oz.) can Reddi Whip real whipped light cream

Using a bread knife, or other serrated knife, slice the cake the long way into three slices. Lay the bottom slice on a nice. serving plate. Cover it evenly with half the ice cream or sherbet. Place the middle section on top and press down firmly. Spread the remaining ice cream or sherbet on this layer and replace the top, pressing down again. "Frost" the cake with the whipped cream. Stick the candles in NOW and freeze till 10 minutes you before you are going to serve the cake. Cut with a sharp knife.

If you want to be a little more gourmet, add fresh or canned fruit to each layer on top of the ice cream or sherbet and save 3-4 to garnish and decorate the top of the cake. Try one or more of these:

Sliced fresh strawberries	Crushed pineapple, drained
Sliced fresh bananas	Peppermint sticks, crushed
Butter Brickle	Mandarin orange sections, drained
Heath bars	Red Hots

Chocolate Towers

*E

Sinfully simple

> **5 large flat chocolate wafer cookies per person**
> **1 can (7 oz.) Reddi Whip real whipped light cream**

Cover a cookie sheet with waxed paper. For each tower start with a cookie, spread with whipped cream, top with another cookie, and repeat till you've used all five cookies. Add a decorative curl of whipped cream to the top and freeze until ready to serve.

Two Minute Magical Mousse

*F&E

Hide the ingredients and make this ahead of time so your guests will never guess how absurdly easy this rich, rich delight really is!

> **1 small package Jell-O instant pudding mix (vanilla or pistachio—unfortunately chocolate doesn't work as well because it stays grainy, but try the suggestion for turning vanilla into mocha.)**
> **2 c. (1 pt.) chilled whipping cream**

Pour the pudding mix into a bowl and stir in the cream with a whisk. Beat the mixture with the whisk until it starts to thicken and spoon into tall glasses, like wine glasses, and place in the ice box to chill until serving time. For a really fancy treat, swirl two kinds of mousse together gently before distributing among the serving glasses.

Mocha Mousse

*F&E

Make vanilla mousse. As the mousse thickens, add coffee concentrate (instant coffee—1 t. dissolved in 1 T. hot water and then cooled) and 2 T. chocolate syrup.

Your Future in Menu Management

Menu Ideas

Sesame Chicken*
Buttered Rice*
Sliced Cucumbers with French Dressing

Fried Shrimp*
Cocktail Sauce*
Au Gratin Potatoes*
Green Beans

Mimosa Chicken*
Corn Bread
Sliced Tomatoes

Surprise Burgers*
Corn on the Cob*
Green Salad with Ranch Dressing

Ham Slice*
Buttered Rice with Parsley*
Pineapple Rings

Sloppy Joes*
French Fries*
Deli Cole Slaw

Minnesota Fish Fry*
Tartar Sauce*
Hash Browns*
Sliced Tomatoes

Pizza—the Works

Basic Burger*
Noodles Romanoff*
Green Salad with Caesar Dressing

Spaghetti with Meat Sauce*
Garlic Roll*
Green Salad with Italian Dressing

Meat Loaf*
Mashed Potatoes*
Green Beans Almondine

Tacos, Ground Beef or Chicken*
Salsa*
Guacamole*

"Stinky" Ribs*
Potato Skins*
Green Salad with Oil and Vinegar Dressing

Pork Chops—Plain*
Macaroni and Cheese
Apple Sauce with Zip*

Linguini Carbonara*
Romaine Salad with Hot Bacon Dressing
Garlic Bread*

Bacon Burgers—the Works

TRUTH: A good hamburger, taco, or pizza is a complete meal—meat, starch, dairy, and vegetable/fruit.

*recipe included

Your Own Favorite Menus

Easy And Expandable After-The-Game Buffet

(For 10 or more)

3 Sour Cream Dips * • Assorted Chips
Oven BBQ Hot Dogs
Baked Beans
Giant Green Salad with Choices of Dressings
Buñuelo Chips (Quarters)

Impress The Guests Dinners

Sweet and Sour Ribs * • Nuked Chinese Nibblers *
Sweet and Sour Sauce
Chinese Mustard
Egg Foo Yung * • Buttered Rice * • Cucumbers
Sesame Chicken *
Whipped Cream Cake with Crushed Pineapple
and Mandarin Orange Wedges *

Chili Con Queso *
Tortilla Chips *
Shrimp Cabrillo *
New Potatoes *
Buñuelos with Vanilla Ice Cream *

Antipasto Plate *
Scampi on Linguini *
Green Salad with Cherry Tomatoes and
Creamy Italian Dressing
Chocolate Towers *

Seafood Spread *
Ritz Crackers
Guacho BBQ Ribs *
Dennis Day Potatoes *
Romaine Salad with Caesar Dressing and Croutons
Vanilla/Mocha Swirl *

An Elegant Buffet Supper

Smoked Salmon Paté * • Ritz Crackers
Lamb Riblets * • Deviled Eggs *
Hot Artichoke Dip * • Triskets
Walking Potatoes *
Cheddachut Spread * • Wheat Thins

Index

Beef
Bacon Burgers 12
Basic Burgers 12
BBQ Short Ribs 30
Chipped Beef Roll-Ups 66
John Marzetti. 14
Lasagna 15
Mega Meatballs 17
Meatloaf. 19
Oven BBQ Guacho Beef Ribs . . . 29
Salisbury Steak. 19
Sloppy Joes. 13
Speedy Spaghetti Sauce 14
Surprise Burgers 12
Taco/Tostada Meat. 17

Casseroles
Everyone's Tuna. 43
Green Bean 58
John Marzetti. 14
Lasagna 15

Chicken
Fried Chicken. 22
Mimosa BBQ Chicken. 21
Oriental Chicken Salad 23
Plain Good (Breasts) 22
Salad. 22
Sesame Chicken. 21
Tacos 23

Desserts
Apple Brown Betty. 72
Buñuelos 71
Chocolate Towers. 73
Mocha Mousse. 73
Rice Pudding 71
Two Minute Magical Mousse . . . 73
Whipped Cream Cake 72

Dips—Cold
Cream Cheese and Olive 64
Guacamole. 69
Sour Cream 64

Dips—Hot
Artichoke. 63
Chili Con Queso 62

Eggs
Boiled. 24
Deviled. 27
Foo Yung 26
Fried. 25
Omelets 26
Poached 25
Salad. 27
Scrambled et al. 26

Fish
Caviar (About). 61
Everyone's Tuna Casserole. 43
Minnesota Fish Fry 42
Salmon Patties 42
Simply Smashing Seafood Spread 67
Shrimp
    Cabrillo. 44
    Fried 43
    Scampi 44
"Smoked" Salmon Paté 65
Tuna Salad 45

Lamb
Lamb Riblets 31

Nibblers
Cheddachut Spread 67
Cheese Crisps. 65
Garlic Bread El Cheapo 70
Gourmet Garlic Bread. 70
Nuked Chinese Nibblers 61
Mexican Pizza 62
Salami Cornucopias. 66
Seasoned Cream Cheese 66
Spiced Pecans. 65
Stack-Ups. 63

Pasta
- Del Mar 49
- Lasagna 15
- Linguini Carbonara 49
- Noodles Romanoff. 50
- Primavera. 49
- Simple Pasta. 48
- Stuffed Pasta 50

Pork
- Basic Bacon 34
- Chinese Sweet & Sour Ribs 31
- Chops—Plain. 35
- Chops—Smothered 36
- Dad's Hot Dog Special. 38
- Ham Salad Imitation 37
- Ham Salad Real 37
- Ham Slice. 36
- Heavenly "Stinky" Pork Ribs 30
- Hot Ham Kabobs. 60
- Nuked Bacon 34
- Nuked Chinese Nibblers 61
- One Dead Hot Dog 60
- Oven BBQ Hot Dogs. 38
- Pigs in a Blanket 39

Salads
- Antipasto 69
- Chicken 22
- Egg 27
- Ham—Imitation 37
- Ham—Real 37
- Oriental Chicken 23
- Tuna. 45

Sauces
- Sauce For Hot Dogs. 38
- Cabrillo 45
- Cocktail 67
- Easy BBQ 29
- Guacamole. 69
- Guacho BBQ 29
- Mean Mustard 68
- Salsa Fresca 68
- Secret Surprise Sauce. 13
- Speedy Spaghetti 14
- Tartar 68

Starches
- Baked Beans. 57
- Baked Potato 52
- Boiled New Potatoes 54
- Corn Fritters 57
- Corn on the Cob 56
- Dennis Day Potatoes 53
- French Fries 54
- Green Bean Casserole 58
- Hashed Browns 55
- Mashed Potatoes 54
- Mexi-Corn 56
- Potatoes Au Gratin. 53
- Potato Salad 54
- Potato Skins 56
- Really Perfect Minute Rice. 52
- Walking Potatoes 61

Family Album

Recipes

Recipes